Lyrical Canvases

Where Poetry Meets Painting

Grayson Rivers

Contents

1 Introduction: A Brush with Words **5**
- 1.1 The Interplay of Art Forms 8
- 1.2 Ekphrasis: Poetry's Embrace of Art 11
- 1.3 Visualizing Verses 14

2 Color as Emotion: Hues of Language **19**
- 2.1 Chromatic Resonance 22
- 2.2 Painting Feelings 25
- 2.3 The Language of Pigments 27

3 Texture and Rhythm: Tactile Verse **31**
- 3.1 The Rhythm of Brushstrokes 34
- 3.2 Textured Wordscapes 36

4 Form and Structure: Canvas and Stanza **41**
- 4.1 Visualizing Poetic Forms 44
- 4.2 Structure in Both Media 47
- 4.3 Parallel Architectures 49
- 4.4 Framing the Narrative 52
- 4.5 The Canvas as a Stage 55

5 Light and Shadow: Illuminating Meaning **59**
- 5.1 Chiaroscuro in Poetry 62
- 5.2 The Play of Light and Dark 65
- 5.3 Illuminating the Unspoken 68

6 Movement and Stillness: Capturing Time 71
6.1 Frozen Moments 74
6.2 The Illusion of Motion 76

7 Beyond the Canvas: Legacy and Inspiration . . . 81
7.1 Inspiring Future Creations 83
7.2 The Enduring Dialogue 86
7.3 A Lasting Symphony 89
7.4 Bridging the Arts 92
7.5 The Power of Synthesis 95

1 Introduction: A Brush with Words

The convergence of poetry and painting isn't a mere intersection; it's a fusion, a vibrant dance where words and images intertwine, creating a richer, more profound artistic experience. Think of a painter meticulously layering colors on a canvas, each stroke adding depth and meaning. Similarly, a poet carefully selects words, crafting verses that evoke not only emotions but also visual sensations. This synergy between visual and literary art forms allows for a unique exploration of human expression, where the canvas becomes a page and the poem a painted masterpiece. We delve into this dynamic interplay, examining how these seemingly distinct disciplines enrich and illuminate one another, fostering a deeper understanding of both. This isn't just about appreciating art; it's about experiencing it on multiple levels, seeing words as colors and images as verses.

Ekphrasis, the act of responding to art through words, isn't simply describing a painting. It's about capturing its essence, translating its visual language into the realm of poetry. Imagine standing before a Van Gogh landscape, the vibrant yellows and blues swirling before you. An ekphrastic poem wouldn't merely list the colors; it would delve into the emotions they evoke, the sense of movement they create, the story they whisper. It's a conversation between the poet and the painting, a dialogue that transcends the boundaries of medium and time. Through ekphrasis, we gain a new perspective on the artwork, unlocking hidden layers of meaning and appreciating its power anew. The poet becomes an interpreter, guiding us through the visual landscape and enriching our understanding of the artist's vision.

Consider the power of visual imagery in poetry. A well-chosen metaphor can paint a picture more vivid than any photograph. A poet might describe a lover's blush as "the faintest rose at dawn," instantly conjuring a delicate hue and a sense of burgeoning emotion. This ability to create mental images is central to the poetic experience, transforming words into brushstrokes that paint scenes within the reader's mind. By carefully selecting words and arranging them with precision, the poet constructs a world that the reader can inhabit, a world rich with color, texture, and emotion. This is where the true magic of poetry lies – in its ability to transcend the limitations of language and evoke a visceral, sensory experience.

Poetry isn't confined to describing visual art; it can also be inspired by it. A painter might use color to convey a particular mood, while a poet might use rhythm and rhyme to achieve the same effect. The interplay between these elements creates a dynamic relationship, where one art form informs and enhances the other. Think of the way a musician might compose a piece inspired by a painting, translating the visual elements into musical notes. Similarly, a poet can draw inspiration from the composition, color palette, and subject matter of a painting, weaving these elements into their own creative tapestry. This cross-pollination of artistic ideas enriches both forms, leading to new and innovative expressions.

The exploration of this interconnectedness between poetry and painting will take us on a journey through various aspects of both disciplines. We'll delve into the nuances of color, texture, form, light, and movement, examining how these elements are employed in both visual and literary art. By understanding the underlying principles that govern these art forms, we can gain a deeper appreciation for the creative process and the power of artistic expression. This isn't just about analyzing techniques; it's about understanding the human impulse to create, to communicate, and to connect with the world around us through the language of art.

We will explore how poets use language to evoke the same emotional responses as painters achieve through color and composition. We'll examine how the structure of a poem can mirror the architecture of a painting, creating a sense of balance and harmony. We'll also consider the role of light and shadow in both art forms, exploring how these elements can be used to create depth, atmosphere, and symbolic meaning. By examining these parallel techniques, we can begin to see the deeper connections between these seemingly disparate disciplines.

Finally, we will explore how the interplay of movement and stillness can be captured in both poetry and painting. Think of a Degas dancer, frozen mid-leap, yet radiating a sense of dynamic energy. A poet might achieve a similar effect through carefully chosen verbs and evocative imagery, creating a sense of motion within the static confines of the page. This ability to capture fleeting moments and imbue them with a sense of timelessness is a testament to the power of art to transcend the limitations of its medium. By exploring these nuanced aspects of artistic expression, we can gain a deeper appreciation for the creative possibilities that lie at the intersection of words and images. This journey through the interwoven worlds of poetry and painting promises to be a rich and rewarding one, offering new insights into the power of art to illuminate the human experience. By embracing the synergy between these two art forms, we can unlock a deeper understanding of both and discover new avenues for creative expression.

1.1 The Interplay of Art Forms

Consider the Sistine Chapel ceiling. Michelangelo's breathtaking frescoes, a swirling narrative of biblical scenes, are a testament to the power of visual storytelling. Now, imagine attempting to capture the grandeur, the emotional weight, the sheer scale of this masterpiece in words. This act of translation, of transforming visual experience into language, is at the heart of the interplay between art forms. It's not simply about description; it's about finding the poetic equivalent of color, texture, composition, and light. It's about understanding how these elements work together to create an emotional impact and then using words to evoke a similar response in the reader. This translation isn't a one-way street. Just as poetry can interpret and illuminate painting, visual art can find inspiration in the rhythms, imagery, and emotional landscapes of poetry.

The dynamic between painting and poetry extends beyond mere subject matter. Think about the concept of color, for instance. A painter might use a vibrant red to convey passion or anger, while a poet might use words like "crimson," "fiery," or "blood-red" to evoke similar emotions. The chosen hue, or its linguistic counterpart, becomes a powerful tool for conveying meaning and shaping the audience's emotional response. Similarly, consider the texture of a painting – the rough impasto of Van Gogh's sunflowers or the smooth, ethereal quality of a Monet water lily. A poet can mirror these textures through carefully selected words, creating a "verbal canvas" that engages the reader's senses. Words like "coarse," "jagged," "silken," or "velvety" become the poet's brushstrokes, adding depth and tactile richness to the poem's imagery. This interplay of texture enriches both the visual and literary experience, creating a richer sensory tapestry.

This cross-pollination of techniques isn't limited to color and texture. The structure of a poem, its stanzas, line breaks, and rhyme scheme, can be seen as analogous to the composition of a painting, its lines, forms, and use of space. A tightly structured sonnet, with its strict rhyme and meter, might mirror the precise, geometric composition of a Renaissance painting, while a free verse poem, with its fluid and unpredictable form, might evoke the more abstract and expressive qualities of a modern artwork. The way a poet arranges words on a page, much like the way a painter arranges elements on a canvas, can direct the audience's attention, create visual or rhythmic patterns, and shape the overall meaning of the work. This parallel in structural approach reveals a deeper connection between these seemingly disparate art forms.

Light and shadow, another crucial element in both painting and poetry, provide further opportunities for interplay. Consider the dramatic chiaroscuro of Caravaggio's paintings, where stark contrasts between light and darkness create a sense of drama and intensity. Poets, too, can employ contrasting imagery of light and dark to evoke specific moods and emotions, using words like "luminescent," "shadowy," "glimmering," or "obscure" to create a similar play of light and shadow within their poems. The strategic use of these contrasting elements adds depth and emotional resonance to both visual and literary art, highlighting the symbolic power of light and darkness to convey complex meanings.

Furthermore, both painting and poetry grapple with the challenge of representing time and motion within a static medium. A painter might use techniques like blurring or implied lines to suggest movement, while a poet might use vivid verbs and dynamic imagery to create the illusion of motion within the confines of the poem's structure. Consider a painting of a galloping horse, where the artist uses blurred lines and dynamic posture to convey the animal's speed and power. A poet might achieve a similar effect through carefully chosen verbs and evocative descriptions of the horse's muscles, mane, and hooves. This shared challenge of capturing movement within a static form fosters creative solutions that enhance the dynamism and impact of both art forms.

Ultimately, the interplay between art forms enriches our understanding and appreciation of each individual medium. By exploring the parallels between poetry and painting, we gain a deeper insight into the creative process and the ways in which artists use different tools and techniques to express their vision. This interdisciplinary approach encourages us to look beyond the surface of a work of art, to consider the underlying principles of composition, color, texture, and form that contribute to its overall impact. It fosters a richer and more nuanced understanding of the artistic language, allowing us to appreciate the subtleties and complexities of both visual and literary expression. This exploration reveals a shared artistic vocabulary that transcends individual mediums, highlighting the interconnectedness of human creativity.

1.2 Ekphrasis: Poetry's Embrace of Art

Ekphrasis, at its core, is a transformative act. It's not merely describing a painting; it's a dynamic interplay, a conversation between two distinct artistic languages. Think of it as translation, not of words from one tongue to another, but of visual elements into the realm of language. Color, texture, composition, light – these become the poet's vocabulary, reshaped and reinterpreted through the lens of their individual perception. A brushstroke of crimson in the painting might become a "fiery slash" in the poem, the rough texture of impasto transformed into "ridged whispers" of paint. This process isn't about replicating the visual experience, but about creating a new, synergistic one. It's about adding another dimension to the artwork, enriching its meaning through a different sensory modality. The poem doesn't exist in isolation; it's intrinsically linked to the artwork, drawing breath from its essence while simultaneously imbuing it with new life. Consider, for example, a poem responding to a landscape painting. The poet might not simply describe the trees, the sky, and the distant mountains. Instead, they might explore the emotional resonance of the scene. The dappled light filtering through the leaves might become a metaphor for memory, the stillness of the lake a reflection of inner peace. The colors themselves, beyond mere description, could evoke specific feelings – the melancholic blue of twilight, the vibrant green of burgeoning life. The poet might also delve into the implied narrative within the painting. Who are the figures depicted, if any? What is their story? What is the artist trying to convey through their chosen subject matter and composition? The ekphrastic poem can explore these questions, weaving a tapestry of words around the visual threads presented by the artist.

This act of interpretation is where the true power of ekphrasis lies. It allows for a deeper engagement with both the painting and the poem, inviting the audience to participate in the creative process. When we read an ekphrastic poem, we're not simply receiving information about a painting. We're being invited to see it through the poet's eyes, to experience it through their unique sensibility. This adds a layer of complexity to our understanding of the artwork, opening up new avenues of interpretation. We might notice details we hadn't seen before, or connect with the painting on an emotional level we hadn't anticipated. The poem becomes a lens through which we can view the artwork anew.

Furthermore, ekphrasis challenges the boundaries between visual and literary art, blurring the lines between seeing and reading, image and word. It reminds us that these art forms are not isolated entities, but rather different facets of the same creative impulse. They speak to each other, inform each other, and enrich each other in profound ways. A successful ekphrastic poem doesn't merely describe the subject of a painting; it engages with its form, its texture, its underlying themes. It probes the very essence of the artwork, seeking to uncover the hidden dialogues between artist and subject, between canvas and viewer.

One crucial element of successful ekphrasis is the poet's ability to find their own voice within the dialogue with the artwork. It's not about mimicking the artist's style or intentions, but about bringing one's own unique perspective to the table. The poem should be a genuine response to the painting, an authentic expression of the poet's individual experience. This might involve focusing on a particular aspect of the painting that resonates deeply, or exploring a theme that emerges from the interplay of visual elements. The poet's voice should be distinct, adding another layer of meaning to the conversation, rather than simply echoing the artist's message.

Moreover, ekphrasis can be a powerful tool for exploring the nature of perception itself. How do we see? How do we interpret what we see? How does language shape our understanding of visual experience? These questions lie at the heart of the ekphrastic endeavor. By translating visual elements into language, the poet illuminates the subjective nature of perception, revealing how individual experiences and interpretations can shape our understanding of the world around us. Each ekphrastic poem is a testament to the power of individual perspective, demonstrating how the same artwork can evoke vastly different responses in different viewers, and how those responses can be articulated through the nuanced and evocative language of poetry.

Finally, consider the emotional impact of ekphrasis. A well-crafted ekphrastic poem can evoke a powerful emotional response in the reader, mirroring the emotional resonance of the artwork itself. By tapping into the sensory details of the painting, the poet can create a visceral experience for the reader, transporting them into the world of the artwork. The poem becomes a bridge between the viewer and the painting, fostering a deeper connection and a more profound appreciation for the power of both visual and literary art. It is in this shared experience, this emotional communion, that the true magic of ekphrasis resides. Through the interplay of words and images, we gain a deeper understanding not only of art, but of ourselves and the world we inhabit.

1.3 Visualizing Verses

Turning the page from the introductory exploration of ekphrasis, we now delve into the practical application of visualizing verses. Think of a poem not merely as a sequence of words, but as a nascent artwork, waiting to be realized on the canvas of your mind. This act of visualization is not about literal depiction, but about capturing the essence, the emotional resonance, the core message that the poem conveys. It's a transformative process, turning abstract concepts into tangible images, breathing life into the poet's words. This process necessitates an understanding of the poem's nuances, its rhythm, and its unique voice.

Consider the use of imagery. A poem describing a "crimson sunset bleeding across the sky" isn't merely providing meteorological information. It paints a picture of vibrant color, of a day's dramatic end, perhaps even hinting at underlying themes of passion or loss. Your visualization should embrace these subtleties, capturing not just the literal red of the sunset, but the emotional weight it carries within the poem's context. Perhaps this translates to bold brushstrokes of scarlet and orange across your mental canvas, or maybe it manifests as a softer, more melancholic blend of hues. The key is to let the poem guide your inner artist.

Metaphor and simile offer further opportunities for visual translation. When a poet compares "love to a red, red rose," they're not suggesting a literal equivalence. They're invoking the rose's beauty, its delicate yet resilient nature, perhaps even its thorns as a symbol of love's complexities. In visualizing this verse, you wouldn't simply paint a rose alongside a heart. Instead, you might explore the textures and colors associated with both love and roses, seeking a visual language that captures the essence of the comparison. Perhaps the velvety petals of the rose translate into a soft, diffused light in your visualized scene, or the thorns might be represented by jagged lines or contrasting textures. The goal is to capture the metaphorical essence, not the literal image.

Sound devices, like alliteration and onomatopoeia, also contribute to a poem's visual potential. The "slippery slither of a snake" not only creates a vivid auditory image, but also suggests a visual representation of sinuous movement and potentially even a sense of danger or unease. Your visualization might focus on the sleek curves of the snake's body, the glistening scales, or the way it blends into its environment. The sound itself should inform the visual, creating a multi-sensory experience within your imagination.

Beyond individual lines and phrases, consider the overall structure and form of the poem. A sonnet, with its strict rhyme scheme and meter, might evoke a sense of order and symmetry, perhaps influencing your visualized scene with balanced compositions and clearly defined forms. Free verse, on the other hand, might inspire a more fluid and abstract visualization, mirroring the poem's lack of rigid structure. The poem's form becomes a framework for your visual interpretation, shaping the overall composition and guiding the flow of your imagined scene.

Furthermore, the poem's emotional tone should heavily influence your visualization. A melancholic poem might evoke muted colors and somber imagery, while a joyful poem might inspire vibrant hues and dynamic compositions. Don't just see the words; feel them. Let the poem's emotional undercurrent guide your visual choices, creating a cohesive and emotionally resonant image in your mind. This emotional connection is crucial for truly understanding and appreciating the poem's deeper meaning.

Practice this technique with a variety of poems. Start with shorter, simpler pieces, gradually working your way up to more complex and challenging works. Experiment with different visualization styles, from realistic depictions to abstract interpretations. The more you practice, the more adept you'll become at unlocking the visual potential hidden within the language of poetry. It's a journey of discovery, a process of unveiling the hidden images that lie dormant within the written word.

Ultimately, visualizing verses is a deeply personal and subjective experience. There's no right or wrong way to do it. The key is to engage with the poem on a deeper level, allowing its words to spark your imagination and guide your inner artist. By transforming poetry into a visual medium, you'll not only enhance your understanding and appreciation of the poem itself but also unlock a new dimension of creative expression within yourself. It's a process of transforming the intangible into the tangible, giving shape and form to the emotions and ideas that lie at the heart of every poem. This act of visualization becomes a bridge between two seemingly disparate art forms, creating a rich and rewarding synthesis of words and images. Through this practice, you'll discover that poetry isn't just something to be read; it's something to be seen, felt, and experienced on a deeply personal and transformative level.

2 Color as Emotion: Hues of Language

We perceive the world through a vibrant spectrum of color, a language as old as light itself. Long before words, color communicated essential information: the ripeness of fruit, the danger of fire, the serenity of a clear sky. This innate understanding of color's significance continues to permeate our emotional and psychological responses. Think of the fiery intensity of red, associated with passion, anger, or danger. Contrast that with the calming embrace of blue, often linked to peace, tranquility, and introspection. This inherent link between color and emotion provides a potent tool for artists working in both visual and literary mediums.

In painting, color is the primary vehicle for conveying emotion. A vibrant splash of yellow can evoke joy and optimism, while a muted palette of grays and blues might suggest melancholy or solitude. The Impressionists, masters of capturing fleeting moments and subjective experiences, understood this implicitly. Monet's use of shimmering blues and greens in his water lilies series evokes a sense of serenity and wonder, while Van Gogh's swirling yellows and oranges in "Starry Night" transmit a palpable sense of energy and emotional intensity. These artists didn't merely depict scenes; they painted feelings.

Poets, too, wield color with precision, using it to paint emotional landscapes with words. They understand the power of "chromatic resonance," the way specific hues can evoke specific emotional responses in the reader. Consider the evocative power of Emily Dickinson's "purple Host" in her poem "I felt a Funeral, in my Brain," a phrase that conjures a sense of regal yet somber grandeur, reflecting the weighty procession of thoughts within her mind. Or visualize the stark contrast between the "black night" and the "white hills" in Robert Frost's "Stopping by Woods on a Snowy Evening," a duality that emphasizes both the beauty and the isolating chill of the winter landscape. The language of pigments translates directly into the language of poetry. Just as a painter carefully selects their palette, a poet chooses words that carry specific chromatic weight. "Azure," "crimson," "emerald," and "gold" – these words are not merely descriptive; they are emotionally charged. They carry within them the cultural and symbolic weight associated with their respective hues, adding layers of meaning and emotional depth to the poetic landscape. A "scarlet" dress might suggest passion and defiance, while a "silver" lining offers a glimmer of hope. The poet, like the painter, utilizes color not simply to decorate, but to illuminate the inner world.

This interplay between color and emotion becomes even more complex when we consider the subjective nature of perception. What one person finds calming, another might find unsettling. Cultural context also plays a significant role in how we interpret color. In some cultures, white symbolizes purity and innocence, while in others it represents mourning and loss. These nuances add depth and complexity to the use of color in both poetry and painting, allowing for a richer, more nuanced exploration of emotional states. The skilled artist, whether working with words or pigments, understands these subtleties and utilizes them to create work that resonates deeply with the viewer or reader.

By carefully selecting and combining colors, poets can create a symphony of emotions, mirroring the techniques used by painters. They can build tension with contrasting hues, create a sense of harmony with analogous colors, or evoke a specific mood through the strategic use of a dominant color. Consider, for instance, the pervasive use of gray in T.S. Eliot's "The Love Song of J. Alfred Prufrock," a color that reflects the poem's themes of alienation and emotional emptiness. The dull, monotonous hues mirror the protagonist's inner landscape, creating a powerful sense of desolation.

Understanding the psychology of color can greatly enhance both the creation and appreciation of art. Warm colors, such as reds, oranges, and yellows, tend to evoke feelings of energy, excitement, and passion. Cool colors, such as blues, greens, and purples, are often associated with calmness, serenity, and introspection. Neutral colors, like browns, grays, and blacks, can convey a sense of stability, grounding, or even melancholy.

However, it's important to remember that these are general associations, and the impact of color is always influenced by context and individual interpretation. The same hue can evoke different emotions depending on its surrounding colors, the subject matter, and the overall tone of the work. A splash of red in a predominantly green landscape might signify danger or a focal point, while a field of red poppies might evoke feelings of remembrance or the ephemeral nature of beauty.

Ultimately, the power of color lies in its ability to evoke a visceral response, to bypass the rational mind and speak directly to our emotions. It's a language that transcends words, a universal language understood across cultures and time. By recognizing and harnessing this power, poets and painters can create works that not only capture the beauty of the visual world but also delve into the depths of human experience, expressing emotions that words alone can sometimes fail to capture. The successful artist learns to wield color not just as a decorative element, but as a powerful tool for storytelling, emotional expression, and the creation of truly resonant and meaningful art. It is in this harmonious blend of color and language, of visual and literary artistry, that the deepest connections are forged and the most profound truths are revealed.

2.1 Chromatic Resonance

Consider the evocative power of crimson. In painting, it can represent passion, rage, or even the quiet blush of budding love. Think of the violent strokes of red in a depiction of a battlefield, contrasted with the delicate flush on a portrait subject's cheek. Now, translate that to poetry. We might use "crimson tide" to evoke the bloodshed of war, or "crimson petals" to suggest the fragile beauty of a flower. The choice of words, their placement within the line, and the surrounding imagery all contribute to the specific shade of meaning we ascribe to the color. This interplay between visual art and the written word is what we call chromatic resonance, the echoing of color's emotional weight across different artistic mediums. It's about capturing the essence of a hue, its visceral impact, and translating it into language that resonates with the reader on a similarly profound level. This translation isn't simply about substituting a color word for its visual counterpart. It requires a deeper understanding of the psychological and cultural associations we have with different hues. Blue, for example, often symbolizes tranquility and peace in Western cultures, yet it can also represent mourning or melancholy. In Eastern cultures, blue can symbolize immortality or healing. Therefore, simply stating "the sky was blue" doesn't harness the full potential of chromatic resonance. Instead, consider "a melancholy blue draped the sky," imbuing the color with a specific emotional weight. Or perhaps, "the vibrant blue of healing waters," using the color to evoke a sense of restoration and hope. The context, the accompanying words, and the overall tone of the piece all influence the final resonance of the chosen color.

Furthermore, chromatic resonance can be amplified by contrasting and combining colors. Consider the effect of placing a vibrant yellow next to a deep violet. The contrast creates a visual vibration, a sense of energy and excitement. This same principle can be applied to poetry. Juxtaposing words associated with these colors – "sun-kissed meadows" against "twilight shadows" – can create a similar sense of dynamic tension within the poem. This interplay of contrasting colors and their associated imagery allows poets to create complex emotional landscapes, mirroring the layered effects achieved by painters on canvas.

Think about the specific shades and tints within a color family. The difference between a scarlet and a maroon, for instance, is more than just a variation in hue. Scarlet pulses with energy, while maroon carries a sense of weight and richness. This subtle nuance in color can be mirrored in word choice. "A scarlet scream tore through the night" conveys a starkly different image than "maroon velvet draped her shoulders." The former suggests raw emotion, while the latter hints at luxury and composure. This attention to the nuances of color, both in painting and poetry, allows artists to create works of profound depth and complexity.

Finally, consider the role of the reader's own experiences and cultural background in interpreting color. While certain color associations may be universal, others are deeply personal. A particular shade of green might remind one reader of a lush childhood garden, while evoking a sense of unease in another. This subjective element adds another layer of complexity to chromatic resonance. The poet can't fully control how the reader will interpret their use of color, but by carefully crafting the surrounding imagery and language, they can guide the reader toward a deeper understanding of their intended meaning. Ultimately, the power of chromatic resonance lies in its ability to evoke a shared emotional experience, a bridge between the visual and the verbal, allowing color to speak in the language of poetry. It is in this intersection of the seen and the felt that art truly comes alive.

2.2 Painting Feelings

Anger simmers, a pot about to boil over. How do you translate that visceral heat onto canvas? Think of jagged lines, slashing brushstrokes of crimson and black, perhaps a distorted figure caught in the throes of this emotional eruption. Consider the way a thick impasto application of paint can mirror the feeling of pressure building, a physical manifestation of the internal struggle. Subtlety can be equally powerful. A muted palette of greys and blues punctuated by a single, vibrant streak of red can convey a sense of controlled fury, the calm before the storm breaks. The key is to connect the internal experience with external expression, allowing the emotion to dictate the visual language.

Joy, on the other hand, bursts forth like fireworks, a kaleidoscope of light and color. Think of swirling brushstrokes, vibrant hues that dance across the canvas. Consider the uplifting effect of yellows and oranges, the invigorating touch of greens and blues. Experiment with textures that reflect the lightness and airiness of joy, perhaps incorporating elements of collage or mixed media to create a sense of celebratory abundance. Imagine the sheer delight of applying paint with abandon, letting the brush dance across the surface, mirroring the effervescent nature of the emotion itself. Let the canvas become a playground of color and light, a visual symphony of pure happiness.

Sadness often manifests as a quiet withdrawal, a retreat into the shadows. Explore the use of muted tones, blues and greys that evoke a sense of melancholy. Think of soft, blurred lines, a gentle wash of color that suggests the ephemeral nature of grief. Negative space can be just as powerful as the painted image, creating a sense of emptiness or loss. Consider the way a single, solitary figure in a vast landscape can convey the isolation and vulnerability that often accompany sadness. The aim is not to replicate the emotion literally, but to create a visual metaphor that resonates with the viewer's own experiences of sorrow.

Fear can be a visceral, gripping sensation, a tightening in the chest, a shortness of breath. Explore the use of sharp, angular lines, distorted figures, and a palette that reflects the physiological responses to fear. Think of the stark contrast of black and white, the jarring effect of unexpected color combinations. Consider the way dripping paint can mimic the feeling of sweat or tears, the way a heavily textured surface can evoke a sense of unease. Experiment with creating a sense of claustrophobia or disorientation through the use of perspective and composition. The goal is to translate the physical and emotional manifestations of fear into a visual language that speaks to the primal nature of this emotion.

Love, in its myriad forms, can be expressed through a variety of visual languages. Think of soft, flowing lines, gentle curves, and a palette that reflects the warmth and tenderness of affection. Consider the use of pinks and reds, the calming influence of blues and greens. Explore the interplay of light and shadow, creating a sense of intimacy and connection. Experiment with textures that evoke the feeling of touch, the softness of skin, the gentle caress of a loved one's hand. The objective is to capture the essence of love, whether it be romantic, familial, or platonic, through a visual expression that resonates with the viewer's own experiences of this complex and multifaceted emotion. Remember, translating feelings onto canvas is not about literal representation, but about finding the visual equivalents of internal states. It's about using color, line, texture, and composition to evoke an emotional response in the viewer, creating a shared experience of feeling. Embrace experimentation, allow yourself to be guided by intuition, and trust the power of art to communicate the complexities of the human heart.

2.3 The Language of Pigments

Pigments possess a language all their own, a vocabulary whispered through hues, saturations, and values. Consider the fiery intensity of cadmium red, a color that speaks of passion, danger, and raw emotion. It's not merely a splotch of color; it's a declaration, a pulsating heartbeat captured on canvas. Contrast this with the serene stillness of cerulean blue, a color that evokes vast skies, tranquil waters, and a sense of boundless peace. The choice of pigment becomes an act of communication, a way for the artist to convey not just what is seen, but what is felt. This interplay between color and emotion forms the very essence of painting's lyrical power, a silent poetry expressed through the vibrant language of pigments.

Understanding this language requires more than simply knowing color names. It necessitates an exploration of the subtle nuances within each hue. Think of the difference between a vibrant, almost luminous, cadmium yellow and the muted, earthy tone of yellow ochre. One shouts for attention, radiating joy and optimism, while the other whispers of age, wisdom, and the quiet beauty of the natural world. Similarly, the coolness of ultramarine blue evokes a different emotional response than the warmth of cobalt blue. One speaks of distant horizons and icy depths, the other of sun-drenched seas and tropical skies. These subtle shifts in tone and temperature contribute to the rich tapestry of emotional expression within a painting, allowing the artist to weave complex narratives through carefully chosen pigments.

Beyond individual colors, the relationships between pigments create another layer of meaning. Complementary colors, like red and green, placed side by side vibrate with an almost electric energy, creating a sense of tension and dynamism. Analogous colors, such as blue, blue-green, and green, flow harmoniously into one another, evoking a sense of calm and unity. The artist, like a poet crafting a verse, carefully orchestrates these relationships, creating visual rhythms and harmonies that resonate with the viewer on a visceral level. The juxtaposition of colors becomes a conversation, a dialogue between hues that adds depth and complexity to the painting's narrative.

Furthermore, the application of paint itself contributes to the language of pigments. A thick, impasto application of paint can create a sense of texture and energy, the brushstrokes themselves becoming a visible record of the artist's emotional state. Conversely, a thin, translucent wash of color can evoke a sense of delicacy and fragility, allowing the light to penetrate the

pigment and create a luminous, ethereal effect. The way the paint is manipulated, layered, and blended becomes an integral part of the painting's expressive language, adding a tactile dimension to the visual experience.
Consider the works of Vincent van Gogh, whose thick, swirling brushstrokes and vibrant palette pulsate with an almost tangible energy. His sunflowers are not merely representations of flowers; they are explosions of yellow, a visual symphony of joy and despair. Contrast this with the serene landscapes of Claude Monet, whose delicate washes of color capture the fleeting light and atmosphere of the French countryside. His water lilies are not simply depictions of a pond; they are meditations on light, reflection, and the ephemeral nature of beauty. These artists, masters of the language of pigments, demonstrate the profound expressive potential of color and its capacity to convey a vast range of human emotions.

The language of pigments extends beyond representation, delving into the realm of symbolism and metaphor. In many cultures, specific colors carry symbolic weight, adding layers of meaning to a painting. Gold, for example, often represents divinity, wealth, and power, while white can symbolize purity, innocence, or mourning, depending on the cultural context. These symbolic associations imbue the painting with a deeper resonance, inviting the viewer to engage with the artwork on multiple levels.

Ultimately, mastering the language of pigments is a lifelong journey of exploration and discovery. It requires not only a keen eye for color and its nuances, but also an understanding of the emotional and symbolic power of each hue. By studying the works of master painters and experimenting with different pigments and techniques, we can begin to unravel the complexities of this visual language and harness its expressive potential in our own creative endeavors. As we deepen our understanding of the language of pigments, we unlock the door to a richer, more nuanced appreciation of the art of painting, allowing us to truly hear the silent poetry spoken by colors. It is in this understanding that we begin to appreciate the full depth and complexity of artistic expression, where color transcends mere decoration and becomes a powerful tool for communication, emotion, and storytelling.

3 Texture and Rhythm: Tactile Verse

Consider the rough surface of a brick wall. Its texture, the uneven mortar, the coarse grit of the brick itself, can be translated into poetry through carefully chosen words. Harsh consonants like 'k' and 't' can mimic the abrupt edges and solidity of the bricks. Short, staccato lines can mirror the fragmented nature of the wall's surface. A poem about such a wall might use words like "jagged," "abraded," or "crumbling" to evoke that specific tactile experience. The poet acts as a translator, converting the physical sensations of texture into a language accessible to the reader's imagination. This translation requires a deep understanding of how words themselves carry inherent textural qualities.

Think of the smooth, cool surface of a polished marble statue. Here, the language shifts. Long, flowing vowels and soft consonants like 'l' and 's' create a sense of fluidity and smoothness. The poem might employ words like "gleaming," "satiny," or "unblemished," inviting the reader to imagine running their hand over the statue's flawless surface. The contrast between the rough brick and smooth marble demonstrates the range of textural possibilities available to the poet. By choosing words with specific sonic qualities and evocative connotations, the writer constructs a palpable experience for the reader, bridging the gap between the visual and the tactile. Rhythm plays a crucial role in creating this textured experience. Just as the rhythm of brushstrokes on a canvas can convey energy, movement, and emotion, the rhythm of a poem can evoke the tactile qualities of a subject. Consider a poem about waves crashing against a rocky shore. The rhythmic pattern of the lines can mimic the ebb and flow of the tide. The use of enjambment, where a sentence continues across a line break, can create a sense of forward momentum, mirroring the relentless advance of the waves. Conversely, a poem about a still, silent forest might employ a slower, more deliberate rhythm, with pauses and caesuras creating a sense of quiet contemplation.

The interplay between texture and rhythm allows the poet to create a truly immersive sensory experience. The rough texture of bark, for example, might be conveyed through harsh consonants and short, choppy lines, while the rustling of leaves could be evoked through a gentle, swaying rhythm. By carefully orchestrating the interplay of these elements, the poet creates a "tactile verse" that engages the reader on multiple levels, inviting them to not only see but also to feel the subject of the poem. This multi-sensory approach to writing deepens the reader's engagement and makes the poem more memorable and impactful.

This concept of tactile verse extends beyond simply describing physical textures. It can also be used to evoke emotional textures. The sharp sting of grief, the warm comfort of love, the prickly unease of anxiety – these emotional states can be translated into tactile experiences through the skillful use of language. A poem about grief might employ jagged rhythms and sharp, cutting words to mimic the rawness of emotional pain. A poem about love might use soft, flowing rhythms and warm, comforting imagery to create a sense of emotional security.

The power of tactile verse lies in its ability to transcend the limitations of language and create a truly immersive experience for the reader. By engaging multiple senses, the poet can evoke a deeper emotional response and create a more lasting impression. Think about how a painter uses layers of paint to create texture on a canvas. Similarly, a poet uses layers of meaning, sound, and rhythm to build a textured wordscape that resonates with the reader long after the poem has been read. This intricate layering of language allows the poem to transcend the purely visual and enter the realm of the tactile, inviting the reader to reach out and touch the very essence of the poem's subject. This fusion of poetic techniques transforms the poem into a multi-sensory experience, blurring the lines between the visual, the auditory, and the tactile. It allows the reader to not just read the poem, but to inhabit it, to feel its textures and rhythms as if they were their own. This powerful connection between poet, poem, and reader is the ultimate goal of tactile verse.

3.1 The Rhythm of Brushstrokes

Consider the act of painting. A loaded brush, brimming with color, meets the canvas. The pressure applied, the direction of the stroke, the speed at which it moves—all contribute to the final visual rhythm. A swift, decisive stroke might convey energy and passion, while a slow, deliberate one suggests contemplation and control. This physical rhythm, born from the artist's gesture, translates into a visual rhythm on the canvas. Think of Van Gogh's swirling, impastoed strokes in "Starry Night," pulsating with a vibrant energy. Contrast that with the smooth, controlled brushwork of a Vermeer, creating a sense of serene stillness. The rhythm isn't merely decorative; it's integral to the emotional impact of the work. It guides the viewer's eye, creating a sense of movement and directing attention to specific areas.

This concept of rhythm translates powerfully to the realm of poetry. Just as brushstrokes build a visual cadence, words create a sonic one. The arrangement of syllables, the rise and fall of intonation, the pauses and enjambments—all these elements contribute to the poem's overall rhythm. A poem with short, clipped lines might feel urgent and energetic, while one with long, flowing lines might evoke a sense of calm or melancholy. Consider the staccato rhythm of a haiku, capturing a fleeting moment in its concise form, versus the expansive rhythm of a free verse poem, allowing for a greater exploration of thought and emotion. This rhythmic interplay shapes not only the sound of the poem but also its meaning, influencing how the reader perceives and interprets the words.

Think of the deliberate use of punctuation. A comma creates a brief pause, a semicolon a longer one, a period a full stop. These pauses, like rests in music, allow the reader to absorb the preceding words and prepare for what follows. Similarly, enjambment, the carrying over of a sentence or phrase from one line to the next without punctuation, creates a sense of forward momentum, propelling the reader through the poem. These techniques, borrowed from musical composition, add layers of complexity and nuance to the poem's rhythm, enhancing its expressive power.

Meter, the patterned arrangement of stressed and unstressed syllables in a line of poetry, further refines the rhythmic landscape. Iambic pentameter, the most common meter in English poetry, creates a steady, heartbeat-like rhythm, lending a sense of formality and elegance. Other meters, such as trochaic and anapestic, offer distinct rhythmic variations, each contributing to the poem's overall tone and effect. The skilled poet manipulates these metrical patterns to create a variety of rhythmic effects, from the gentle lull of a lullaby to the driving force of a war chant.

Beyond the mechanics of meter and punctuation, the choice of words themselves plays a crucial role in establishing rhythm. The sounds of the words, their inherent musicality, contribute to the overall sonic texture of the poem. Assonance, the repetition of vowel sounds, and consonance, the repetition of consonant sounds, create internal rhymes and echoes, enriching the poem's rhythmic complexity. These sonic devices, employed strategically, can evoke specific moods and emotions, adding another layer of meaning to the words themselves.

Consider the use of alliteration, the repetition of consonant sounds at the beginning of words, in a line like "While I nodded, nearly napping." The repeated "n" sound creates a drowsy, lulling effect, perfectly mirroring the sense of nodding off to sleep. Or consider the use of assonance in a line like "The rain in Spain falls mainly on the plain." The repeated "ai" sound creates a sense of openness and space, mimicking the vastness of the plain. These subtle sonic details, often operating on a subconscious level, contribute significantly to the poem's overall impact.

Ultimately, the rhythm of a poem, like the rhythm of a painting, is more than just a surface feature. It's an integral part of the work's meaning, shaping how we perceive and interpret it. By understanding the nuances of rhythm, both visual and sonic, we can gain a deeper appreciation for the artistry of both painting and poetry. We can begin to see how these seemingly disparate art forms, through their shared attention to rhythm, can offer a richer, more nuanced understanding of the world around us. They offer a glimpse into the artist's mind, revealing their unique perspective and emotional landscape. By attuning ourselves to these rhythms, we open ourselves to a deeper, more resonant experience of art.

3.2 Textured Wordscapes

Consider the surface of a weathered brick wall. Its rough, pitted texture, imprinted with the passage of time, offers a tangible sense of history, a story whispered in the language of erosion and decay. Now, imagine translating that tactile experience into words. Not simply describing the wall's appearance, but evoking its very essence—the coolness of its shadowed crevices, the gritty resistance under your fingertips, the way light catches the edges of broken mortar. This is the power of textured wordscapes in poetry, the art of using language to create a sensory experience that transcends the visual and enters the realm of touch.

Achieving this tactile quality involves a careful selection of words and a keen awareness of their inherent sensory connotations. Think about the difference between saying "smooth stone" and "polished obsidian." The latter, with its sharper consonants and evocative imagery, conjures a more specific and tangible sensation. The poet's toolbox is filled with such tools: assonance and consonance, the subtle interplay of vowel and consonant sounds, can mimic the rustling of leaves or the grating of sand. Onomatopoeia, the use of words that imitate sounds, brings the world to life with the crackle of fire or the whisper of wind.

Beyond individual words, the arrangement of phrases and lines contributes to the overall texture of a poem. Short, staccato lines can create a sense of abruptness or roughness, mirroring the jagged edges of a broken rock face. Conversely, long, flowing lines can evoke the smooth undulation of a silken fabric. Enjambment, the continuation of a sentence without a pause beyond the end of a line, can create a sense of momentum and fluidity, like water cascading over smooth stones. The poet, like a sculptor, shapes the very form of the poem to reflect the textures they wish to evoke.

Metaphor and simile, those cornerstones of poetic language, play a crucial role in building textured wordscapes. Comparing a lover's touch to velvet or a harsh word to sandpaper immediately imbues the abstract with a tangible quality. These comparisons draw on the reader's own sensory experiences, creating a bridge between the poem and the physical world. By grounding abstract concepts in concrete imagery, the poet allows the reader to not just understand, but to feel the emotions and ideas being conveyed.

Sensory details are paramount. Don't just tell the reader that a forest is dark; describe the way the shadows cling to the moss-covered bark, the damp earth yielding beneath their feet, the scent of pine needles filling the air. The more specific and evocative the details, the more fully the reader is transported into the poem's world. This immersive quality is what distinguishes a truly textured wordscape from a mere description.

Consider the use of synesthesia, a literary device that blends different senses. Describing a sound as "sharp" or a color as "loud" creates a surprising and often powerful sensory effect. By blurring the lines between the senses, the poet invites the reader to experience the world in a new and unexpected way. This intermingling of sensory perceptions can heighten the tactile experience, making the wordscape even more vivid and memorable.

Revisiting the example of the brick wall, think about how you might evoke its texture through the lens of another sense. Perhaps the "silence of aged brick" speaks to the way sound is absorbed by its porous surface. Or perhaps the "sun-baked scent of clay" hints at the material's origins. By engaging multiple senses, even indirectly, you enrich the textual experience and create a more layered and complex wordscape.

Furthermore, consider the role of negative space. Just as a sculptor chips away at stone to reveal the form within, a poet can use carefully chosen omissions to enhance the tactile qualities of their work. By leaving certain details unsaid, they invite the reader to fill in the gaps with their own sensory experiences, creating a more personal and intimate connection with the poem. The unsaid can be just as evocative as the said, adding another layer of texture to the wordscape.

Ultimately, crafting textured wordscapes is about more than just using descriptive language. It's about creating an immersive sensory experience for the reader. It's about choosing words not just for their meaning, but for their sound, their rhythm, their ability to evoke touch, taste, smell, and sound. It's about transforming language into a tactile medium, a way of reaching out and touching the reader's very soul. Through the skillful manipulation of language, the poet can build worlds that are not just seen, but felt, tasted, smelled, and heard. They create a symphony of sensations that resonate long after the poem has been read, leaving the reader with a lingering sense of having touched something real, something tangible, something profoundly moving.

4 Form and Structure: Canvas and Stanza

Consider the canvas, a rectangular or square plane, a defined space within which the painter creates. This boundary, seemingly restrictive, actually provides a framework for infinite possibilities. It dictates the outer limits of the composition, forcing the artist to consider how every element relates to the edges and to each other within that specific area. Similarly, the stanza in poetry serves a similar function. Whether a tight sonnet or a sprawling free verse composition, the stanza provides a container for a specific thought, image, or emotional progression. It's a unit of meaning, a building block in the larger architecture of the poem, mirroring the way individual elements within a painting combine to create a unified whole. Think of a haiku, its seventeen syllables a miniature canvas, demanding precise placement of each word for maximum impact. Just as the painter chooses the size and shape of their canvas, the poet selects the form and structure that best suits their expression.

This interplay between form and structure becomes even more evident when we consider specific poetic forms. The sonnet, with its fourteen lines and intricate rhyme scheme, can be likened to a carefully composed still life, each element precisely placed and balanced within the frame. The strictness of the form encourages a density of meaning, much like the careful arrangement of objects in a still life painting. Conversely, free verse, unbound by traditional rules, might be compared to an abstract expressionist painting, allowing for greater fluidity and spontaneity. The poet, like the abstract painter, explores the possibilities of space and rhythm, creating a visual and auditory experience through the arrangement of words on the page. The white space around and between lines becomes as important as the words themselves, mirroring the negative space in a painting that gives shape and definition to the subject.

Parallel architectures exist within both media. The golden ratio, a mathematical principle found throughout nature, has been used by both painters and architects for centuries to create harmonious and aesthetically pleasing compositions. Poets, too, albeit perhaps less consciously, often utilize similar principles of balance and proportion when structuring their work. The placement of line breaks, the length of stanzas, and the overall flow of the poem can create a visual rhythm that echoes the golden ratio's inherent harmony. The placement of a caesura, a pause within a line of poetry, can create a focal point similar to the way a painter uses light to draw the viewer's eye to a particular area of the canvas. These structural choices, whether made instinctively or with deliberate intent, contribute to the overall impact and meaning of the work.

Framing, both literal and figurative, plays a crucial role in shaping narrative. A painter uses the frame of the canvas to define the boundaries of their world, to focus the viewer's attention on the scene within. The poet achieves a similar effect through the use of titles, epigraphs, and dedications, which act as a frame around the poem, providing context and setting the stage for the reader's experience. Within the poem itself, the poet might employ techniques like enjambment, carrying a sentence or phrase over from one line to the next, to create a sense of movement and anticipation, guiding the reader's eye down the page much like a winding path through a landscape painting.

Consider the canvas as a stage, and the painted elements as the actors in a play. The composition dictates the relationships between these actors, their proximity and positioning creating a narrative, a frozen moment in time. Similarly, the stanza in poetry functions as a scene, containing a specific moment or interaction. The arrangement of lines within the stanza, the use of enjambment or end-stopped lines, creates a rhythm and pacing that mirrors the unfolding action on a stage. Just as a director carefully stages a scene to emphasize certain elements and create dramatic tension, the poet uses form and structure to highlight key images, emotions, and ideas, guiding the reader's experience and shaping the overall impact of the poem. The white space around the stanza, like the wings of a stage, provides a space for reflection and anticipation, allowing the reader to absorb the scene before moving on to the next.

4.1 Visualizing Poetic Forms

Consider the sestina, a complex dance of six repeating end-words across six stanzas, culminating in a three-line envoi. Visualize its structure as a spiral, each stanza a chamber radiating from a central core. The spiraling movement mimics the cyclical return of the end-words, creating a sense of both progression and recurrence. A painter might represent this through a circular canvas, with the end-words inscribed in segments, their paths intertwining like threads of color. Think of the envoi, the final three lines, as the spiral's culminating point, where all the threads converge, a burst of color at the center. This visual representation captures the sestina's intricate structure, its tightly woven web of words.

Now, shift your focus to the sonnet. Its fourteen lines, traditionally divided into an octave and a sestet, can be envisioned as a diptych, a two-paneled artwork. The octave, presenting the problem or theme, might be represented by a landscape bathed in shadow, evoking a sense of mystery or conflict. The sestet, offering the resolution or reflection, could then transition into a brighter landscape, the same scene now illuminated, symbolizing understanding or acceptance. This visual divide mirrors the sonnet's structural shift, its movement from proposition to resolution. The painter's use of light and shadow reinforces the poem's thematic arc, creating a visual echo of its internal logic. Imagine a distinct line separating the two panels, perhaps a streak of gold leaf, emphasizing the turning point within the poem.

The haiku, with its concise seventeen syllables arranged in three lines, demands a different visual approach. Imagine a single brushstroke, a swift arc of ink on a blank canvas. This minimalist aesthetic captures the haiku's essence, its focus on a single, fleeting moment. The three segments of the brushstroke, varying in length and intensity, mirror the haiku's syllabic structure. This visual representation emphasizes the haiku's brevity and immediacy, its ability to encapsulate a world within a few carefully chosen words. The vast expanse of white space surrounding the brushstroke further amplifies the poem's sense of isolation and contemplation, mirroring the meditative quality often found in haiku.

Consider the free verse poem, its unbound form flowing organically across the page. Visualize this as a Jackson Pollock splatter painting, a chaotic yet harmonious explosion of color. The absence of rigid structure in the poem is reflected in the seemingly random distribution of paint, yet within this apparent disorder lies a deeper meaning. The varying densities of color, the intersecting lines, the subtle shifts in texture, all correspond to the poem's internal rhythms, its emotional peaks and valleys. This visual interpretation captures the free verse poem's dynamic energy, its refusal to be confined by traditional forms. The painter's spontaneous gestures mirror the poet's freedom of expression, creating a visual equivalent of the poem's untamed spirit.

Finally, envision the villanelle, with its intricate repetition of two rhyming refrains, as a tapestry. The recurring lines, woven throughout the poem's nineteen lines, can be represented by threads of contrasting colors, their repeated appearance creating a visual pattern. These threads intertwine with other threads, representing the evolving narrative, forming a rich and complex design. The final quatrain, where both refrains converge, can be visualized as the tapestry's culminating point, a knot where all the threads are tightly bound together. This visual representation highlights the villanelle's cyclical nature, its intricate interplay of repetition and variation. The tapestry's interwoven threads mirror the poem's carefully constructed architecture, its delicate balance of familiarity and surprise. This exercise in visualization not only illuminates the structural intricacies of various poetic forms, but also opens up new avenues for creative expression, inviting us to explore the fertile ground where poetry and painting intersect. By translating the abstract structures of poetry into concrete visual forms, we gain a deeper appreciation for the artistry of both mediums, and discover new ways to interpret and engage with the power of language and image. This process of visualization encourages a more holistic understanding of art, bridging the gap between the seen and the heard, the painted and the spoken. It invites us to experience poetry not just through the ear, but also through the eye, enriching our appreciation for its intricate beauty and enduring power. By learning to see poetic forms, we unlock a new dimension of understanding, expanding our capacity to appreciate the artistry of language.

4.2 Structure in Both Media

Consider the architectural underpinnings of a poem laid beside the compositional structure of a painting. A sonnet, with its rigid fourteen lines and prescribed rhyme scheme, mirrors the carefully constructed composition of a Renaissance painting, perhaps a portrait where the subject is precisely placed within the frame, adhering to the rule of thirds. The sonnet's volta, that crucial turn in thought in the final sestet, can be likened to a shift in perspective within the painting, a subtle change in lighting or a gesture that redirects the viewer's gaze. Just as the artist uses lines and shapes to create balance and harmony, the poet uses meter and rhyme to achieve a similar effect, building a framework that supports the emotional and intellectual weight of the poem. This structural resonance creates a sense of order and elegance, inviting the audience to appreciate the artistry of both forms.

Free verse, on the other hand, with its fluid structure and lack of prescribed rules, finds its counterpart in abstract expressionism. Think of a Jackson Pollock painting, with its chaotic drips and splashes of color, mirroring the unpredictable flow of thought and emotion in a free verse poem. The absence of traditional structure doesn't signify a lack of form; rather, it represents a different kind of architecture, one built on intuition and spontaneity. The poet, like the abstract expressionist painter, embraces the freedom to explore the complexities of human experience without the constraints of traditional forms. The structure emerges organically from the poem's internal logic, creating a dynamic interplay between form and content.

Visualize a haiku, a concise seventeen-syllable poem that captures a fleeting moment in nature. Its minimalist structure echoes the simplicity and elegance of a Japanese ink painting, where a few brushstrokes evoke an entire landscape. Both forms prioritize economy of expression, distilling complex ideas and emotions into their purest essence. The haiku's three lines, like the carefully placed elements in an ink painting, create a sense of balance and harmony, inviting the viewer/reader to contemplate the profound beauty of the natural world. This shared emphasis on brevity and precision allows both forms to achieve a powerful impact with minimal means.

Now, shift your focus to the narrative structure within a longer poem, perhaps an epic or a ballad. Compare it to the narrative unfolding within a history painting, a genre that depicts significant historical events. Both forms utilize structure to guide the audience through a story, creating a sense of progression and development. The poet uses stanzas and cantos to organize the narrative, while the painter uses compositional elements to direct the viewer's eye through the scene. The careful arrangement of figures, the use of perspective, and the interplay of light and shadow all contribute to the unfolding narrative, just as the poet's use of imagery, metaphor, and symbolism enhances the story's impact.

Consider the frame of a painting, the boundary that defines the artwork's space and separates it from the surrounding world. This frame can be likened to the stanza in a poem, the container that holds the lines of verse and gives them shape. Just as the frame focuses the viewer's attention on the artwork within, the stanza provides a framework for the poet's thoughts and emotions. It creates a sense of closure and completeness, allowing the reader to pause and reflect on the meaning of the words. The stanza break, like the edge of the canvas, provides a moment of respite, a space for the reader to breathe before moving on to the next thought.

Finally, imagine the canvas as a stage, a space where the artist orchestrates a visual drama. Similarly, the page becomes a stage for the poet, a space where words perform and interact. The poet uses language to create characters, set scenes, and evoke emotions, much like a playwright. The arrangement of words on the page, the use of line breaks and white space, all contribute to the poem's dramatic effect, creating a sense of movement and rhythm that engages the reader's imagination. Just as the actors on a stage bring a play to life, the poet's words animate the page, transforming it into a vibrant and dynamic space.

4.3 Parallel Architectures

Consider the architectural blueprints of a poem and a painting. While seemingly disparate mediums, they share a common language of structure. In poetry, this structure manifests in stanza length, meter, and rhyme schemes. Think of the rigid framework of a sonnet, its fourteen lines locked into a specific rhyme scheme and rhythm. This pre-determined structure acts as a container for the poem's emotional and thematic content, shaping how the reader experiences the unfolding narrative or emotional arc. Similarly, a painter uses the canvas as their architectural plane. The dimensions of the canvas, the placement of figures and objects within the frame, and the use of lines and perspective all contribute to the overall composition and impact of the work. A long, horizontal canvas might evoke a sense of expansiveness, while a small, square canvas might create a feeling of intimacy. Just as an architect uses lines and angles to define a building's form, poets and painters employ lines and shapes to create structure within their respective art forms. A painter might use strong diagonal lines to create a sense of movement and dynamism, or converging lines to draw the viewer's eye to a focal point. In poetry, line breaks can be used to create pauses and emphasis, mirroring the visual breaks created by lines in a painting. The placement of words within a line, or the length of the lines themselves, can create a visual rhythm that complements the poem's meaning. Consider the stark, minimalist poetry of Ezra Pound, where the placement of individual words on the page takes on immense significance. This mirrors the precision and economy of line found in Japanese ink painting, where a single brushstroke can convey volumes.

Furthermore, both poetry and painting utilize the concept of framing to direct the viewer/reader's attention and create a sense of unity. A painter uses the edges of the canvas to define the boundaries of the artwork, creating a frame within which the visual elements are contained. This frame acts as a window into the artist's vision, focusing the viewer's gaze on the scene or subject depicted. In poetry, the stanza acts as a type of frame, containing a specific unit of thought or emotion. The white space surrounding a stanza, much like the frame of a painting, separates it from other stanzas and allows it to stand as a distinct unit within the larger structure of the poem. Think of the villanelle, with its repeating lines and refrains acting as both internal and external frames, creating a circular, almost claustrophobic sense of structure.

The deliberate arrangement of elements within a defined space is crucial to both poetry and painting. A painter carefully considers the placement of figures, objects, and colors within the composition to create balance, harmony, or tension. This arrangement guides the viewer's eye through the painting, creating a visual narrative or emotional experience. Similarly, a poet arranges words, lines, and stanzas to create a specific effect on the reader. The ordering of words within a line affects the rhythm and flow of the poem, while the arrangement of lines within a stanza creates a visual pattern that contributes to the overall meaning. Consider the carefully constructed stanzas of a pantoum, where lines are repeated and rearranged to create a sense of echoing and layering. This careful orchestration of elements within the confines of the form mirrors the deliberate composition of a painting.

Consider the sonnet form again. Its strict structure, with its prescribed rhyme scheme and meter, can be seen as analogous to the precise dimensions and proportions of a classical painting. Just as the artist works within the constraints of the canvas, the poet works within the constraints of the sonnet form, finding creative ways to express complex ideas and emotions within a pre-determined framework. This parallel architecture provides a sense of order and control, allowing both artist and poet to focus their creative energies within a defined space. Just as a cathedral's arches and buttresses support its soaring structure, so too do the structural elements of a poem or painting provide a framework for its artistic expression. This inherent structure, whether visible or implied, allows the artwork to stand on its own, a testament to the careful craftsmanship of its creator. The understanding of these parallel architectures deepens our appreciation for the artistry involved in both poetry and painting, revealing the intricate interplay between form and content that lies at the heart of both art forms. It allows us to appreciate not only the beauty of the finished work, but also the skill and intentionality that went into its creation.

4.4 Framing the Narrative

Narrative structure in poetry, much like the composition of a painting, provides a framework for understanding the interplay of elements within the artwork. Think of a canvas: before the paint touches the surface, the artist considers the dimensions, the orientation, and the overall shape of the canvas itself. This preliminary act of framing dictates the boundaries within which the narrative will unfold, influencing how the viewer perceives the final image. Similarly, in poetry, the chosen form—be it a sonnet, a haiku, or free verse—establishes the initial parameters for the poem's narrative. The constraints and freedoms inherent in each form guide the poet's choices regarding rhyme scheme, meter, and stanza length, ultimately shaping the reader's journey through the poem's landscape.

Consider the distinct impact of a tightly structured sonnet compared to the fluid nature of free verse. The sonnet, with its fourteen lines and prescribed rhyme scheme, creates a sense of contained narrative, often focused on a single theme or emotional arc. This inherent structure encourages a concentrated exploration of the subject matter, demanding precision and economy of language. Free verse, on the other hand, offers greater flexibility, allowing the narrative to meander and expand organically, mirroring the unpredictable currents of thought and experience. The poet's decision to employ a specific form becomes an integral part of the narrative itself, influencing the pacing, tone, and overall impact of the poem.

Framing also extends to the deliberate sequencing of images and ideas within a poem. Just as a painter arranges figures and objects on the canvas to create a specific visual narrative, the poet orders words and images to guide the reader's emotional and intellectual response. The placement of a particular image or metaphor can dramatically alter its significance within the larger context of the poem. A vivid image at the beginning might establish a dominant tone, while a subtle shift in imagery towards the end can create a lingering sense of ambiguity or resolution. This purposeful arrangement of elements, akin to the composition of a painting, contributes to the overall narrative flow and thematic coherence of the poem.

Perspective, a crucial element in both painting and poetry, plays a vital role in framing the narrative. In painting, the artist's chosen perspective—whether bird's-eye view, close-up, or something in between—shapes the viewer's understanding of the scene. Similarly, in poetry, the speaker's perspective, or point of view, acts as a lens through which the narrative is filtered. The choice of first-person, second-person, or third-person narration significantly impacts the reader's connection to the poem's emotional core. A first-person narrative offers an intimate glimpse into the speaker's inner world, while a third-person perspective provides a broader, more objective view of the narrative events.

Moreover, the poet's choice of diction, tone, and imagery contributes to the framing of the narrative. Just as the painter's palette influences the mood and atmosphere of a painting, the poet's language shapes the reader's emotional response. The use of vivid, sensory language can immerse the reader in the poem's world, while stark, minimalist language can create a sense of detachment or introspection. The poet's skillful manipulation of these linguistic tools allows for nuanced control over the narrative's emotional impact, adding layers of meaning and complexity.

Finally, the concept of negative space, often utilized in visual art, finds a parallel in poetry. In painting, negative space refers to the areas surrounding the main subject, contributing to the overall composition and balance of the image. In poetry, negative space can manifest as strategic silences, omissions, or gaps in the narrative. These deliberate omissions invite the reader to actively participate in the meaning-making process, filling in the gaps with their own interpretations and experiences. This interplay between what is explicitly stated and what is left unsaid creates a dynamic tension, enriching the poem's narrative depth. By understanding the principles of framing, both poets and painters alike can craft compelling narratives that resonate with their audience on multiple levels. The deliberate choices regarding form, structure, perspective, and language contribute to a cohesive and impactful artistic experience.

4.5 The Canvas as a Stage

Consider the canvas not just as a surface for paint, but as a stage for a narrative. Every element placed upon it—every line, every splash of color, every subtle shift in texture—becomes a player in a visual story. Just as a playwright carefully constructs a scene, the artist arranges these elements to guide the viewer's eye, creating a sense of drama, movement, and emotion within the confines of the frame. Think of how a spotlight isolates an actor on stage, drawing the audience's attention to their expression or gesture. Similarly, the strategic use of light and shadow in a painting can highlight a particular area, emphasizing its importance within the overall composition. This interplay of elements transforms the static surface into a dynamic space, inviting the viewer to participate in the unfolding narrative. This concept of the canvas as a stage is particularly relevant when considering the intersection of poetry and painting. A poem, like a play, unfolds through time, revealing its narrative through a sequence of words and images. When we approach the canvas with this theatrical mindset, we can begin to see how the principles of staging can be applied to visual art. The arrangement of figures, the use of perspective, and the manipulation of light and shadow all contribute to the creation of a visual narrative that resonates with the poem's themes and emotional trajectory. Imagine a painting inspired by a poem about loss. The artist might use muted colors, elongated figures, and a sense of emptiness in the composition to mirror the poem's melancholic tone.

The placement of figures within the composition is crucial to this staging process. Just as actors move across a stage, interacting with each other and the set, the figures in a painting create a dynamic interplay within the frame. Their positions, postures, and gestures communicate relationships, emotions, and the unfolding narrative. A painting depicting a lively market scene might feature a multitude of figures engaged in various activities, creating a sense of bustling energy and social interaction. Conversely, a portrait focusing on a solitary figure might emphasize introspection and contemplation through the subject's posture and gaze. The artist becomes a director, orchestrating the scene to convey the desired emotional impact.

Perspective also plays a vital role in this visual storytelling. Just as a stage set creates an illusion of depth and space, perspective in a painting draws the viewer into the scene, creating a sense of three-dimensionality on a flat surface. By manipulating vanishing points and lines of convergence, the artist can control the viewer's journey through the image, guiding their eye towards key elements and shaping their understanding of the narrative.

Imagine a landscape painting with a winding path leading towards a distant horizon. The use of perspective creates a sense of depth and invites the viewer to imagine themselves walking along that path, experiencing the journey firsthand.

Color, too, becomes a powerful tool in this theatrical approach to painting. Just as stage lighting can create different moods and atmospheres, the artist's choice of colors can evoke specific emotions and enhance the overall narrative. Warm, vibrant colors might convey joy and celebration, while cool, muted tones might suggest sadness or contemplation. Think of a painting inspired by a poem about nature's vibrant energy. The artist might use a palette of rich greens, blues, and yellows to capture the poem's sense of vitality and abundance. The interplay of light and shadow further enriches the visual narrative, adding depth, drama, and symbolic meaning. Just as a spotlight isolates an actor on stage, the strategic use of light in a painting can highlight a particular area, emphasizing its importance within the overall composition. The contrast between light and shadow can also create a sense of mystery or intrigue, inviting the viewer to explore the hidden depths of the image.

Texture, often overlooked, contributes significantly to the canvas's stage-like presence. The rough texture of impasto, where paint is thickly applied, can convey a sense of energy and movement, while smooth, blended surfaces might suggest tranquility and stillness. The tactile quality of the paint itself becomes an integral part of the narrative, adding another layer of meaning and emotional resonance. Imagine a seascape painting where the artist uses thick impasto to depict the crashing waves, creating a visceral sense of the ocean's power.

By approaching the canvas as a stage, artists can transform a static surface into a dynamic space, inviting viewers to engage with the narrative unfolding before them. This theatrical approach to painting enriches the interplay between visual and literary art, allowing the canvas to become a powerful vehicle for storytelling and emotional expression. The careful arrangement of elements, the use of perspective, color, light, shadow, and texture all contribute to the creation of a visual experience that resonates deeply with the viewer, just as a well-staged play captivates its audience. The canvas becomes a world unto itself, a stage where stories are told and emotions are brought to life through the interplay of artistic elements. It's a space where the viewer is not merely an observer but an active participant in the unfolding narrative, invited to explore the depths of meaning and emotional resonance that the artist has carefully crafted.

5 Light and Shadow: Illuminating Meaning

Consider the interplay of light and shadow in the world around us. Observe how the sun, filtering through leaves, creates dappled patterns on the forest floor, or how a single streetlamp etches sharp lines against the night. These natural occurrences offer a rich vocabulary for poets seeking to imbue their work with depth and meaning. Just as a painter utilizes chiaroscuro to model form and create dramatic contrast, so too can a poet employ contrasting imagery of light and darkness to illuminate the emotional landscape of a poem. This technique isn't merely about describing the visual; it's about using light and shadow as metaphors, as emotional anchors.

Think of light as representing hope, clarity, revelation, or joy, while shadow embodies fear, doubt, mystery, or grief. This symbolic interplay can be subtle, like the faint glimmer of hope in an otherwise bleak landscape, or stark, like the blinding flash of insight that shatters a period of darkness. The key lies in understanding the emotional weight these elements carry and wielding them with precision. Imagine a poem about loss, where the only source of light is the flickering candle beside a photograph, casting long, dancing shadows on the wall. This single image, laden with both light and shadow, speaks volumes about the fragile nature of memory and the lingering presence of the departed.

Furthermore, the interplay of light and shadow can be used to create a sense of ambiguity, inviting the reader to interpret the meaning beneath the surface. A character bathed in shadow might not necessarily represent evil, but rather a hidden vulnerability or a complex inner world. A ray of light piercing through darkness could symbolize a sudden realization or a fleeting moment of clarity amidst confusion. This ambiguity allows for a richer, more nuanced reading experience, encouraging active participation from the reader. Explore the potential of half-light, the subtle gradations between illumination and obscurity, where meanings become fluid and open to interpretation. This twilight zone, where clarity blurs with mystery, offers fertile ground for poetic exploration.

The manipulation of light and shadow can also contribute significantly to the atmosphere of a poem. A poem set in a brightly lit carnival can evoke feelings of exuberance and excitement, while a poem shrouded in darkness might evoke a sense of unease or foreboding. Consider the effect of moonlight filtering through a stained-glass window, casting multicolored shadows across a room. This image creates a sense of magic and mystery, transforming the ordinary into the extraordinary. This interplay of light and shadow can transform mundane settings into something extraordinary, imbuing them with emotional resonance. The poet becomes a painter with words, crafting a visual experience for the reader through carefully chosen imagery.

Remember, the goal isn't simply to describe light and shadow, but to use them to reveal something deeper about the subject of the poem. If you're writing about a character struggling with internal conflict, you might use contrasting imagery of light and shadow to represent the opposing forces within them. A character wrestling with a difficult decision might be depicted standing at a crossroads, half their face illuminated, the other half shrouded in darkness. This visual metaphor powerfully conveys the internal struggle without resorting to explicit explanation.

Finally, consider the way light and shadow interact with other sensory details in your poem. The sound of rain falling on a sunlit windowpane creates a different emotional effect than the sound of rain falling on a darkened street. The smell of freshly cut grass in the bright morning sun evokes a different feeling than the same smell in the cool evening shade. By weaving together these sensory details with your imagery of light and shadow, you can create a truly immersive and unforgettable reading experience.

Think of the famous painters who masterfully used light and shadow – Caravaggio, Rembrandt, Vermeer. Study their works, not just for the visual impact, but for the storytelling inherent in their use of chiaroscuro. How does the light draw your eye? How does the shadow create a sense of depth and mystery? Translate these observations into your poetry. Imagine a poem inspired by a Rembrandt painting, where a single shaft of light illuminates a figure in a dimly lit room. How can you capture that same dramatic contrast, that same sense of intimacy and revelation, in your words? Observe how light transforms throughout the day, from the soft glow of dawn to the harsh glare of midday to the long shadows of twilight. Each phase of light carries its own unique emotional weight, offering a rich palette for the poet to explore. Consider the reflective qualities of light on different surfaces – the gleam of sunlight on water, the sparkle of a jewel in candlelight, the dull sheen of moonlight on stone. Each variation adds another layer of meaning to your imagery.

5.1 Chiaroscuro in Poetry

Consider the interplay of light and shadow, not merely as visual elements, but as potent tools for shaping meaning and evoking emotion within a poem. Just as a painter uses chiaroscuro to create depth and drama on canvas, so too can a poet manipulate contrasting imagery to illuminate the complexities of the human experience. Darkness, for instance, can represent the unknown, fear, or despair, while light can symbolize hope, revelation, or clarity. By juxtaposing these opposing forces, a poet can craft a powerful emotional resonance within their work, drawing the reader into the nuanced interplay between these contrasting elements. Think of the shadowy depths of a forest contrasted with a single ray of sunlight piercing through the canopy, or the stark brightness of a streetlamp against the inky blackness of a night sky. These visual contrasts create an immediate emotional response, a sense of mystery, or perhaps a glimmer of hope amidst despair. The concept of chiaroscuro extends beyond simple visual descriptions. It can also be employed metaphorically to represent internal conflicts, moral ambiguities, or the shifting tides of emotion. A character grappling with inner demons might be depicted as caught between the light of reason and the shadows of temptation. A poem exploring the theme of loss could utilize imagery of fading light to symbolize the gradual erosion of memory or the dimming of hope. This metaphorical application of light and shadow allows for a more layered and nuanced exploration of complex themes, adding depth and richness to the poetic landscape. It's not simply about describing light and dark; it's about using these elements to illuminate the hidden corners of human experience, revealing the intricate interplay of opposing forces that shape our lives.

Furthermore, the manipulation of light and shadow can be used to control the reader's focus and create a specific mood or atmosphere. A poem bathed in soft, diffused light might evoke a sense of tranquility and peace, while a poem dominated by harsh contrasts and deep shadows could create a feeling of unease or foreboding. The poet, like a skilled cinematographer, can use these elements to direct the reader's gaze, highlighting certain details while obscuring others, creating a sense of mystery or suspense. This deliberate use of light and shadow allows the poet to craft a specific emotional experience for the reader, immersing them in the world of the poem and guiding their interpretation of its meaning. The reader becomes an active participant in the unfolding narrative, their emotional responses shaped by the carefully orchestrated play of light and dark.

Think of the works of poets like Sylvia Plath, whose poetry often employs stark contrasts of light and shadow to explore themes of despair and resilience. Or consider the evocative imagery of Langston Hughes, who used the interplay of light and darkness to depict the complexities of the African American experience. These poets, and countless others, demonstrate the power of chiaroscuro to elevate poetry beyond mere description, transforming it into a visceral and emotionally charged exploration of the human condition. They use light and shadow not just as decorative elements, but as integral components of their poetic language, imbuing their words with a depth and resonance that transcends the purely visual.

Examining the use of chiaroscuro in poetry reveals the profound interconnectedness between visual and literary art forms. Both rely on the manipulation of light and shadow to create depth, evoke emotion, and shape meaning. By understanding the principles of chiaroscuro, aspiring poets can gain valuable insights into how to craft more impactful and evocative verse. They can learn to use contrasts of light and dark to create dynamic imagery, explore complex themes, and engage their readers on a deeper emotional level. This understanding of light and shadow as more than just visual elements, but as powerful tools for shaping meaning, unlocks a whole new dimension of poetic expression, allowing for a richer and more nuanced exploration of the human experience. It is in this interplay between light and dark that the true power of poetry lies, its ability to illuminate the hidden corners of our world and reveal the beauty and complexity that resides within.

5.2 The Play of Light and Dark

Consider the interplay of light and shadow in a painting. A beam of sunlight cutting through a darkened room, illuminating dust motes dancing in the air, instantly creates a focal point, a story whispered in the contrast. This same principle applies to poetry. The strategic use of contrasting imagery, juxtaposing light and darkness, can imbue a poem with depth, mystery, and emotional resonance. Think of it as verbal chiaroscuro, painting with words to illuminate the unspoken.

Darkness, for instance, needn't represent solely negativity. It can symbolize the unknown, the fertile ground of creativity, the quiet introspection where ideas germinate. It can be a comforting blanket, a sheltering embrace against the harsh glare of the world. A poem steeped in shadow can evoke a sense of mystery, inviting the reader to explore the hidden depths of meaning. Imagine a poem describing a moonless night, the rustling of unseen creatures in the undergrowth, the faint glimmer of stars barely piercing the velvet black. The absence of light becomes a presence in itself, a palpable force shaping the reader's experience.

Conversely, light can represent clarity, revelation, hope, or even stark exposure. A sudden burst of light in a poem, like a spotlight on a stage, can draw attention to a specific image or emotion. Consider a poem about a sunrise, the gradual lifting of darkness revealing the vibrant colors of the landscape, a metaphor for the emergence of hope after a period of despair. The contrast between the preceding darkness and the burgeoning light am-

plifies the emotional impact, creating a powerful sense of transformation.
The interplay between light and darkness isn't merely about visual description; it's about creating a sensory experience for the reader. Think about the tactile qualities associated with light and shadow. The coolness of shade on a summer day, the blinding glare of sunlight reflecting off snow, the warm glow of a candle flame. By incorporating these sensory details, you can draw the reader deeper into the poem's world, allowing them to feel the poem as much as they read it.
Furthermore, the use of light and shadow can create a sense of movement and drama within a poem. Imagine a poem describing a flickering candle flame, the shadows dancing on the walls, creating an illusion of life and motion. This dynamic interplay of light and shadow can add a layer of visual interest and emotional intensity, heightening the reader's engagement with the poem.
Consider the symbolic weight that light and shadow can carry. Light often represents knowledge, truth, and spiritual awakening, while darkness can symbolize ignorance, fear, or the unconscious. By playing with these symbolic associations, you can add layers of meaning to your poetry, inviting the reader to interpret the interplay of light and dark on a deeper, more personal level. A single ray of light piercing through the darkness can become a powerful symbol of hope and resilience.
Don't be afraid to experiment with different shades and intensities of light and darkness. A poem doesn't have to be entirely bright or entirely dark; it can contain a spectrum of shades, just like a painting. Think about the

subtle gradations of twilight, the soft glow of moonlight, the deep shadows cast by a midday sun. These nuances can add depth and complexity to your poetry, creating a richer and more evocative reading experience.

Explore the use of figurative language to enhance the interplay of light and shadow. Metaphors, similes, and personification can add a layer of symbolic meaning and emotional depth. For instance, comparing the darkness to a velvet curtain can evoke a sense of mystery and anticipation. Describing the sunlight as "kissing the earth" can add a touch of warmth and intimacy. Remember, the goal isn't simply to describe light and darkness; it's to use them as tools to create mood, atmosphere, and meaning. Think about how the interplay of light and shadow can contribute to the overall theme and message of your poem. Does it symbolize a struggle between good and evil? A journey from ignorance to enlightenment? The complexities of human emotion?

Finally, consider the impact of light and shadow on the reader's emotional response. How do you want them to feel when they read your poem? Do you want to evoke a sense of peace and tranquility? Or do you want to create a feeling of unease and tension? By carefully manipulating the interplay of light and shadow, you can guide the reader's emotional journey, creating a powerful and memorable experience. Through mastering this technique, you transform words into pigments, your poem into a luminous canvas.

5.3 Illuminating the Unspoken

Silence. A canvas untouched, a poem unwritten. Both pregnant with potential, brimming with unspoken stories yearning for release. This chapter explores the profound power of suggestion, the art of conveying meaning through what is not explicitly stated, the resonance of the unsaid in both poetry and painting. Think of the negative space around a sculpted figure, the deliberate absence of detail that draws the eye and amplifies the impact of what is present. Similarly, in poetry, the unspoken can reverberate with a power that surpasses direct expression.

Consider the evocative power of implication. A painter might depict a single, wilting flower in a vase, leaving the narrative of loss and decay to unfold in the viewer's mind. The viewer completes the story, drawing upon personal experiences and associations to imbue the image with deeper meaning. Likewise, a poet might allude to a past event without explicitly describing it, relying on the reader's intuition and imagination to fill in the gaps. This active participation of the audience – whether viewer or reader – creates a more intimate and powerful connection with the artwork. It invites contemplation and encourages a personalized interpretation that resonates on a deeper emotional level.

The use of symbolism further enhances the power of the unspoken. A recurring motif, a carefully chosen color, or a strategically placed object can carry layers of meaning without needing explicit explanation. A painter might use the symbolism of a raven to evoke themes of death or prophecy, while a poet might employ the image of a barren tree to represent loss or despair. These symbolic representations tap into a shared cultural understanding, allowing the artist to communicate complex ideas with economy and grace. The unspoken becomes a language in itself, rich with nuanced meaning accessible to those who understand its subtle vocabulary.

Ambiguity, often perceived as a weakness, can be a powerful tool for illuminating the unspoken. By leaving certain elements open to interpretation, the artist empowers the audience to engage more actively with the work. A painting with blurred lines or obscured figures invites the viewer to complete the image in their mind's eye. A poem with multiple possible readings encourages the reader to explore different interpretations and discover their own unique understanding of the text. This ambiguity allows for a multiplicity of meanings, enriching the experience and fostering a deeper connection between the artwork and the audience.

Silence itself can be a potent form of expression. In painting, a vast expanse of empty canvas can evoke feelings of isolation, vastness, or tranquility. In poetry, the strategic use of pauses and line breaks can create a sense of anticipation, reflection, or emotional weight. The silence becomes a canvas upon which the unspoken can be projected, allowing the audience to fill the void with their own thoughts and emotions. It's in these quiet moments, in the spaces between words and brushstrokes, that the most profound meanings often reside.

Metaphor and simile, powerful tools in both poetry and painting, offer another avenue for illuminating the unspoken. A painter might use the visual metaphor of a caged bird to represent confinement or oppression. A poet might employ the simile "like a ship lost at sea" to convey a sense of disorientation or vulnerability. These figurative devices allow the artist to communicate complex ideas through evocative comparisons, enriching the meaning and deepening the emotional impact of the work. The unspoken is revealed through the lens of analogy, inviting the audience to draw connections and uncover hidden layers of significance.

Ultimately, illuminating the unspoken is about creating a space for dialogue between the artwork and the audience. It's about inviting participation, encouraging interpretation, and fostering a deeper understanding of the complexities of human experience. By mastering the art of suggestion, artists can tap into the power of the unsaid and create works that resonate long after the last brushstroke is applied or the final word is written. It's in these unspoken spaces that art truly comes alive, inviting us to complete the narrative and discover the hidden depths of meaning within.

6 Movement and Stillness: Capturing Time

The artist's challenge lies in capturing the ephemeral, the fleeting moment, and translating it onto a static surface. Consider a dancer mid-leap, a bird taking flight, a wave crashing on the shore. These are instances of dynamic energy, of time unfolding. Yet, the painter, much like the poet, must find a way to freeze these moments, to imbue their canvas or page with the very essence of motion. They strive to create an illusion, a suggestion of movement within the confines of a still frame. This interplay between movement and stillness forms a fundamental tension in art, a paradox that fuels creativity.

Think of Edgar Degas' ballet dancers. Caught in mid-pirouette, their bodies appear suspended, yet we sense the momentum, the impending continuation of the movement. He achieved this not through literal depiction, but through masterful use of line, color, and composition. The angles of their limbs, the flow of their costumes, the blurred edges – all contribute to a sense of dynamism, of captured motion. Similarly, a poet might use enjambment, carrying a phrase across lines without punctuation, to mimic the continuous flow of a dancer's movement. The words themselves become a choreography of meaning, mimicking the physical act on the page.

Consider the opposite: the stillness of a contemplative figure, a quiet landscape, a sleeping child. While seemingly devoid of movement, these subjects possess a different kind of energy, a latent potential. A painter might emphasize this stillness through the use of horizontal lines, muted colors, and a balanced composition. Think of Andrew Wyeth's "Christina's World," the isolated figure yearning for something beyond her reach, the landscape stretching out, vast and still. The very lack of physical movement amplifies the emotional weight of the scene, the internal struggle of the subject. A poet, in turn, might use carefully chosen words and precise imagery to evoke a sense of profound quietude, creating a space for reflection and introspection. The brevity of haiku, for instance, can encapsulate a moment of stillness with remarkable intensity.

The passage of time itself can be depicted through the subtle suggestion of change. A wilting flower, a setting sun, the weathering of stone – these images speak to the inexorable march of time, even within a static artwork. Consider the Dutch Masters' still life paintings. While seemingly static arrangements of fruit and flowers, they often contain subtle hints of decay, reminders of the transient nature of beauty. A browning apple, a drooping petal, a fly buzzing near a piece of overripe fruit – these details introduce an element of time, a sense of impending change. Similarly, a poet can use metaphor and symbolism to evoke the passage of time, comparing human life to the seasons, the ebb and flow of tides, or the slow erosion of a mountain.

Capturing time also involves capturing the emotional resonance of a moment. A fleeting expression of joy, a sudden surge of grief, the quiet contemplation of a memory – these are moments that can be as fleeting as a bird in flight, yet they hold immense power. A skilled artist can capture these emotions not just through facial expressions or body language, but through the overall mood and atmosphere of the artwork. Think of Edward Hopper's paintings, capturing the quiet loneliness of urban life. The figures are often still, yet the paintings are imbued with a sense of longing, of isolation, conveyed through the use of light, color, and composition. A poet might achieve the same effect through evocative language, using words to create a specific emotional tone, to transport the reader to that precise moment in time.

The artist's canvas or the poet's page becomes a stage on which the drama of time unfolds. Whether depicting dynamic action or profound stillness, the goal is to capture the essence of a moment, to make it resonate with the viewer or reader long after the initial encounter. This requires not just technical skill, but a deep understanding of how to manipulate the elements of their chosen medium – line, color, composition, rhythm, and imagery – to create the desired effect. The true mastery lies in making the static dynamic, in capturing the ephemeral dance of time within the confines of art.

6.1 Frozen Moments

Consider the dancer, poised mid-leap, muscles taut, a story unfolding in the arc of her body. A painter captures this ephemeral moment, transforming dynamic energy into a static image. Similarly, the poet, wielding words like brushstrokes, can freeze this same instant, preserving the dancer's fleeting grace within the confines of a verse. This is the power of capturing a frozen moment—to distill the essence of movement and stillness into a timeless artifact. Think of Edgar Degas's ballerinas, their delicate forms caught in a perpetual state of suspended animation, each brushstroke a testament to the ephemeral beauty of their performance.

The challenge lies in translating the fluidity of motion into a fixed medium. How do we, as artists working with words or pigments, convey the sense of a breath held, a muscle contracted, a gesture completed, all within the static confines of a canvas or a page? The answer resides in understanding the subtle interplay of elements that suggest movement even within stillness. Consider the angle of a limb, the direction of a gaze, the ripple of fabric—these details, meticulously rendered, imbue the frozen moment with an echo of the preceding action and the anticipation of what is to come. It is the pregnant pause, the moment of suspended animation that holds the greatest potential for expressive power.

In poetry, we can achieve this through vivid verbs that imply movement even in their past tense form: "leaped," "spun," "stretched." Adverbs contribute further, adding nuance to the action: "swiftly," "gracefully," "effortlessly." The careful selection of these words paints a mental image of the movement itself, allowing the reader to reconstruct the dynamic action within their imagination. We are not simply describing a static pose; we are evoking the kinetic energy that created it. Imagine a poem describing a hummingbird, wings blurred in a frenzy of motion, yet captured in a single, vibrant image through the precise use of language.

Furthermore, the use of imagery can be incredibly effective in suggesting movement within stillness. A wind-rippled flag, a blur of falling leaves, the cascading spray of a waterfall—these images, though frozen in the moment of their description, carry within them the inherent sense of motion. They invite the reader to participate in the experience, to fill in the gaps and reconstruct the dynamic reality that the static image represents. Think of a photograph of a wave just before it crashes, the crest curled and poised, the power contained within that single frame speaks volumes about the dynamic forces at play.

Contrast also plays a crucial role in capturing frozen moments. The stillness of a figure against a bustling background, for example, can amplify the sense of suspended animation. This juxtaposition highlights the figure's isolation from the surrounding activity, drawing attention to the singularity of the captured moment. Equally, the stillness of a landscape can be dramatically enhanced by the presence of a single element in motion—a bird in flight, a lone cloud drifting across the sky. The contrast creates a tension that emphasizes both the stillness and the movement, enriching the overall impact of the scene.

Consider a poem describing a lone figure standing on a windswept beach. The figure is motionless, yet the wind whips around them, creating a sense of dynamic energy. The contrast between the figure's stillness and the wind's movement highlights the frozen moment, making it all the more poignant. This interplay of stillness and motion, of frozen moment and implied dynamism, allows us to capture the essence of fleeting moments and preserve them for eternity, whether on canvas or within the lines of a poem. The art lies in finding the balance, in using the tools of our craft to breathe life into stillness, and to find the eternity within a fleeting instant.

6.2 The Illusion of Motion

The depiction of motion in a static medium like painting or poetry presents a unique challenge. It requires the artist to create an illusion, a suggestion of movement within the confines of a still image or the fixed lines of a verse. Think of Edgar Degas's ballet dancers, captured mid-pirouette, their limbs a blur of pastel, or a horse, frozen mid-gallop in a Romantic landscape. These images don't actually move, yet they convey a powerful sense of dynamism, of captured motion. Similarly, consider the rush of a river described in a poem, the tumbling of leaves in the wind, or the quick, darting flight of a bird. These word-paintings evoke movement through careful selection of verbs, the use of rhythmic language, and the creation of vivid, sensory details. The illusion of motion relies on suggesting the moments just before and just after the captured instant, implying a trajectory, a continuation beyond the frame or the stanza.

One key technique in creating this illusion is the strategic use of lines and forms. In painting, diagonal lines inherently suggest movement and instability, as opposed to the static nature of horizontal and vertical lines. A tilted horizon, a leaning figure, or the sweeping curve of a brushstroke can all contribute to a sense of dynamism. In poetry, this translates to the use of enjambment, where a line breaks mid-phrase, carrying the reader's eye and momentum to the next line, creating a sense of forward motion. Similarly, the use of varied line lengths and rhythmic patterns can mimic the acceleration and deceleration of physical movement. Think of the short, sharp lines used to depict a sudden action, contrasted with the longer, flowing lines that might describe a graceful, flowing motion. This interplay of line and rhythm adds another layer to the illusion, mirroring the dynamic nature of the movement being portrayed.

Blurring and suggestion also play a crucial role in conveying motion. Painters might use blurred lines or softened edges to indicate speed and movement, as seen in Impressionist paintings of bustling city streets or moving trains. The effect creates a sense of fleetingness, capturing a moment in transition. Poets, on the other hand, achieve a similar effect through the use of evocative language, hinting at movement rather than describing it explicitly. A glimpse of a dress disappearing around a corner, the rustling of leaves implying a breeze, or the faint echo of footsteps – these fragmented images create a sense of movement just beyond the reader's grasp, encouraging active participation in imagining the scene. The power of suggestion lies in its ability to engage the reader's imagination, allowing them to fill in the gaps and complete the illusion of motion.

Furthermore, the depiction of motion often relies on capturing a specific moment of transition, a point of change within a larger sequence of actions. This could be the apex of a jump, the moment a wave crests, or the instant a bird takes flight. By focusing on these transitional moments, the artist highlights the dynamic forces at play, implying the preceding and subsequent actions. The viewer or reader is invited to reconstruct the full sequence of movement, to imagine the flow of action that extends beyond the captured moment. This creates a sense of implied movement, extending the illusion beyond the static confines of the artwork.

Contrasting stillness with implied motion can further enhance the illusion. By juxtaposing a moving element against a static background, the artist emphasizes the dynamism of the moving subject. Imagine a single falling leaf against a backdrop of still trees, or a lone figure running across a vast, empty landscape. This contrast amplifies the sense of motion, drawing the viewer's eye to the dynamic element and highlighting the difference between movement and stillness. In poetry, this might involve using static imagery to frame a dynamic moment, such as describing a bustling marketplace against the backdrop of unchanging mountains. This juxtaposition creates a tension between movement and stillness, enriching the overall impact of the piece. The stillness serves as a foil, highlighting the dynamism of the moving element and making the illusion of motion even more compelling. Through these combined techniques, artists create a powerful sense of movement within the constraints of a static medium, transforming the still canvas or the fixed lines of poetry into a dynamic expression of life and energy.

7 Beyond the Canvas: Legacy and Inspiration

The echoes of artistic conversations reverberate through time. Consider the Pre-Raphaelites, deeply influenced by the poetic romanticism of Keats and Tennyson. Their paintings, imbued with literary symbolism and a yearning for idealized beauty, reflect a direct engagement with the themes and aesthetics of their poetic contemporaries. This cross-pollination wasn't a one-way street. Poets, in turn, found inspiration in the Pre-Raphaelite's vibrant canvases, often responding with ekphrastic verses that further explored the narratives and emotions depicted in the paintings. This dynamic exchange enriched both art forms, creating a tapestry of interconnected meaning that continues to resonate with audiences today. The legacy of this exchange serves as a powerful testament to the enduring dialogue between word and image.

This artistic kinship extends far beyond specific movements. Think of the Symbolists, who sought to express abstract ideas and emotions through both poetry and painting. Artists like Odilon Redon, with his dreamlike imagery and evocative use of color, found a natural affinity with the symbolic language of poets like Charles Baudelaire and Stéphane Mallarmé. Their shared exploration of inner landscapes and the subconscious pushed the boundaries of artistic expression, blurring the lines between the visual and the literary. This shared pursuit of meaning through metaphor and symbolism fostered a rich interplay between the two disciplines. The Symbolist movement exemplifies how artists working in different media can find common ground in their exploration of complex themes.

Inspiration can also spring from unexpected sources. The abstract expressionists, with their emphasis on gesture and emotion, drew inspiration from the improvisational nature of jazz music. Poets like Frank O'Hara, immersed in the New York art scene of the mid-20th century, captured the energy and immediacy of abstract expressionism in his poems. His work, much like the paintings of Jackson Pollock or Willem de Kooning, embraced spontaneity and rejected traditional notions of form and structure. This connection between abstract expressionism and poetry highlights the fluidity of artistic inspiration and the potential for cross-disciplinary fertilization. These unexpected connections reveal the interconnectedness of artistic expression.

The dialogue between poetry and painting is not confined to the past. Contemporary artists continue to find inspiration in this dynamic interplay. Consider the work of visual artists who incorporate text into their paintings, creating a layered experience that engages both the eye and the mind. Similarly, poets today often draw inspiration from visual art, responding to specific works or broader artistic movements in their writing. This ongoing exchange demonstrates the enduring power of this interdisciplinary conversation. The contemporary art world thrives on this continuous exchange, ensuring the legacy of interconnected creativity.

Ultimately, the exploration of poetry and painting together reveals a fundamental truth about the nature of art itself: its ability to transcend boundaries and connect us to something larger than ourselves. Whether it's the vibrant colors of a canvas evoking a specific emotion or the rhythmic flow of words painting a vivid image in our minds, both art forms offer a unique window into the human experience. This power to transcend individual disciplines lies at the heart of artistic expression. By engaging with both poetry and painting, we gain a deeper appreciation for the interconnectedness of human creativity and the myriad ways in which art can enrich our lives. The fusion of these two forms offers a profound and multifaceted artistic experience.

7.1 Inspiring Future Creations

The convergence of poetry and painting has a ripple effect, extending far beyond the individual artist and resonating through time to inspire future generations. Consider the Pre-Raphaelites, a brotherhood of painters and poets in 19th-century England, deeply influenced by the vibrant colors and detailed realism of early Italian art. Their works, both visual and literary, often featured intertwined narratives of mythology, religion, and nature, creating a richly layered tapestry of art that continues to captivate audiences today. Their legacy lies not just in their specific creations, but in the demonstration of a potent cross-disciplinary approach that fueled their artistic vision. They established a precedent for exploring the interwoven nature of different artistic mediums.

This cross-pollination of ideas is evident in countless examples throughout history. Think of the profound influence of Japanese woodblock prints, with their flattened perspectives and bold use of color, on Impressionist and Post-Impressionist painters. Artists like Van Gogh and Monet absorbed these aesthetic principles, adapting them to their own Western sensibilities and thereby forging new artistic pathways. This exchange didn't remain solely within the realm of painting; it spilled over into literature, informing the imagery and descriptive language of poets like Ezra Pound and Amy Lowell, who found inspiration in the evocative simplicity of Japanese aesthetics. The inspiration flowed both ways: Western art, in turn, influenced Japanese artists, creating a dynamic feedback loop of creativity.

This dynamic exchange demonstrates that artistic inspiration isn't a one-way street; it's a continuous dialogue. The act of creation itself becomes a conversation across disciplines, where artists borrow, adapt, and transform ideas from each other. The boundaries between art forms blur as artists draw inspiration from diverse sources, leading to the emergence of hybrid forms and innovative approaches. The Symbolist movement, for instance, provides a powerful illustration of this interconnectedness. Poets like Baudelaire and Rimbaud explored the suggestive power of language, using symbols and metaphors to evoke complex emotions and abstract ideas. This emphasis on symbolism resonated deeply with painters like Moreau and Redon, who created visually rich and enigmatic works that mirrored the poets' exploration of the subconscious and the spiritual realm.

Furthermore, the legacy of these interdisciplinary exchanges resides not merely in the finished artworks but also in the creative processes themselves. By engaging with other art forms, artists develop new ways of seeing and thinking. A poet studying the compositional techniques of a painter may discover fresh approaches to structuring a poem. A painter analyzing the rhythmic patterns of a poem may find new ways to express movement and energy on canvas. This reciprocal influence fosters a deeper understanding of the underlying principles of art, regardless of the medium. It promotes a more nuanced appreciation for the elements of composition, the use of color and light, and the expression of emotion. In this sense, the study of one art form enhances and enriches the practice of another.

Moving forward, artists can actively cultivate this interdisciplinary approach to fuel their own creative endeavors. Visiting art museums, attending poetry readings, and engaging with other forms of artistic expression can spark new ideas and broaden perspectives. Exploring the works of artists who have successfully bridged different mediums can provide valuable insights and inspiration. Imagine a contemporary poet studying the abstract expressionist paintings of Mark Rothko, finding inspiration in the interplay of color and form to craft a poem that evokes similar emotions and sensations. Or a sculptor exploring the dynamic rhythms of a musical composition, translating the auditory experience into a three-dimensional form.

In conclusion, the enduring legacy of artistic synthesis lies in its capacity to spark new creative endeavors, to foster cross-disciplinary understanding, and to enrich the artistic landscape as a whole. By embracing the interconnectedness of the arts, we can unlock new possibilities for expression, interpretation, and appreciation. The fusion of poetry and painting, in particular, serves as a powerful reminder of the transformative potential of art, its ability to transcend boundaries, and its enduring power to inspire future creations. This continuous dialogue between art forms, across time and cultures, ensures the vitality and evolution of artistic expression, offering a boundless wellspring of inspiration for generations to come. This cross-pollination of artistic concepts and techniques fuels the creative process and leads to innovative and thought-provoking works of art that continue to challenge and inspire. The exploration of diverse art forms cultivates a deeper understanding of artistic principles and allows artists to discover new avenues for expression. By embracing this interdisciplinary approach, artists can tap into a vast network of creative influences, fostering a richer and more dynamic artistic landscape for the future.

7.2 The Enduring Dialogue

The conversation between poetry and painting isn't a static relic of the past; it's a vibrant, ongoing exchange. This dialogue transcends specific historical periods and artistic movements. It's a fundamental human impulse to connect visual and verbal expression, to find correlations between the seen and the articulated. Think of the prehistoric cave paintings, imbued with narrative power, whispering stories through ochre and charcoal. Those early marks, both representational and symbolic, served as a precursor to both written language and visual storytelling. They represent an innate human desire to capture experience, both inner and outer, through creative acts. This primordial connection underlines the enduring nature of the dialogue between image and word. We see it echoed throughout history, in illuminated manuscripts, religious iconography, and the decorative arts, where words and images intertwine to convey complex narratives and spiritual truths.

Consider the Renaissance, a period of vibrant artistic cross-pollination. Painters like Botticelli drew inspiration from classical mythology, bringing literary narratives to life on canvas. Poets, in turn, responded to the visual richness of these works, crafting verses that further elaborated on their themes and symbolism. This reciprocal relationship fueled a cycle of creativity, enriching both art forms. Michelangelo, a master of both sculpture and poetry, provides a powerful example of this symbiotic relationship. His sonnets, often exploring themes of love, beauty, and artistic creation, resonate with the emotional intensity and physicality of his sculptures. He used both mediums to grapple with similar existential questions, demonstrating the inherent interconnectedness of his artistic vision.

The Romantic poets, deeply moved by the power of nature, found parallels in the landscapes depicted by painters like Caspar David Friedrich. Friedrich's dramatic portrayals of solitary figures amidst vast, sublime landscapes mirrored the Romantic preoccupation with individual experience and the emotional power of the natural world. Wordsworth's poetry, for example, often echoes the sense of awe and wonder evoked by Friedrich's paintings, creating a sense of shared emotional terrain between the two art forms. The poets sought to capture the same sense of awe and transcendence in their verse, contributing to a shared artistic vocabulary that spoke to the spirit of the age.

Modernist artists, grappling with a rapidly changing world, explored new ways of representing reality. Painters like Picasso fractured form and perspective, reflecting the fragmented nature of modern experience. Poets like T.S. Eliot, responding to the same cultural shifts, experimented with fragmented narratives and disjunctive imagery in their work. The disruption of traditional forms in both mediums mirrored the disruption of established social and cultural norms, creating a sense of shared aesthetic rebellion. This shared exploration of fragmentation and abstraction demonstrates the enduring dialogue between poetry and painting, even in the face of radical artistic innovation.

This ongoing exchange extends beyond specific movements and historical periods. It continues to resonate in contemporary art, where artists often blur the lines between disciplines. Conceptual artists, for instance, often incorporate text into their visual works, challenging traditional notions of authorship and artistic medium. Poets, similarly, experiment with visual elements in their work, incorporating typography, graphic design, and even multimedia components to expand the boundaries of the poetic form. This cross-pollination fuels a dynamic and evolving conversation, pushing the boundaries of both art forms and enriching our understanding of the creative process.

The enduring dialogue between poetry and painting isn't simply a matter of imitation or illustration. It's about exploring the shared territory of human experience, the intersection of perception and expression. It's about recognizing the inherent limitations of a single medium and the potential for a more holistic understanding through synthesis. When a poem captures the essence of a painting, or a painting embodies the spirit of a poem, something new and profound emerges. A richer, more nuanced understanding of the creative impulse is revealed, demonstrating the power of art to transcend boundaries and illuminate the human condition. This synergy isn't just about creating beautiful works of art; it's about expanding our capacity for empathy, understanding, and connection with the world around us. It's a testament to the enduring power of human creativity to explore the depths of human experience and to forge connections across time, culture, and artistic boundaries.

7.3 A Lasting Symphony

The echoes of a brushstroke reverberate in the cadence of a verse. The vibrant hues of a canvas find their counterpart in the rich tapestry of poetic language. This enduring dialogue between poetry and painting, this symphony of words and images, extends beyond mere inspiration; it fosters a profound understanding of the creative process itself. By exploring the intersections of these two seemingly disparate art forms, we uncover the universal language of human expression, a language that transcends the limitations of any single medium. We find that the act of creation, whether with brush or pen, is rooted in a shared impulse to capture and convey the essence of experience.

Consider the painter meticulously layering colors, building textures, and shaping light to evoke a specific mood or convey a narrative. The poet, similarly, crafts words, carefully selecting sounds and rhythms, arranging lines and stanzas to create a parallel emotional and intellectual landscape. Both artists are engaged in a process of translation, transforming their inner visions into tangible forms that can be shared with others. This act of translation requires a deep sensitivity to the nuances of their respective mediums, an understanding of how color can resonate with emotion, how rhythm can embody movement, and how structure can shape meaning. This shared pursuit of translating inner experience into external form is what unites the painter and the poet, creating a shared artistic heritage that spans centuries and cultures.

This legacy of shared inspiration is not a static entity; it's a dynamic, ever-evolving conversation between artists across time and space. Think of the Romantic poets, deeply moved by the dramatic landscapes and emotional intensity of painters like Caspar David Friedrich. Their poems, in turn, became a source of inspiration for later generations of artists, creating a continuous feedback loop of creative exchange. This reciprocal influence is evident in countless examples throughout art history, demonstrating the profound interconnectedness of these seemingly distinct disciplines. By studying the ways in which poets have responded to visual art, and how painters have been influenced by literary works, we gain a deeper appreciation for the multifaceted nature of artistic creation.

The power of this synthesis lies in its ability to broaden our perspectives and deepen our engagement with the world around us. When we encounter a poem inspired by a painting, or a painting that echoes the themes of a poem, we are invited to experience these works through a new lens. We see the familiar with fresh eyes, uncovering hidden layers of meaning and appreciating the subtle nuances that might have otherwise gone unnoticed. This cross-pollination of artistic ideas enriches not only our understanding of individual works but also our appreciation for the broader cultural context in which they were created. It encourages us to seek connections, to draw parallels, and to explore the rich tapestry of human creativity in all its diverse forms.

This enduring dialogue, this "lasting symphony," speaks to the fundamental human need to connect with something larger than ourselves. Whether we are moved by the vibrant colors of a Van Gogh landscape or the evocative imagery of a Neruda poem, we are participating in a shared human experience. We are engaging with the world through the lens of art, allowing ourselves to be transported to other times and places, to experience different perspectives, and to connect with the emotions and ideas that resonate across cultures and generations. This is the true power of art – its ability to bridge divides, to foster empathy, and to remind us of our shared humanity.

Furthermore, the intersection of poetry and painting offers a unique opportunity for personal growth and creative exploration. By engaging with these art forms in a thoughtful and intentional way, we can cultivate our own creative sensibilities and expand our capacity for self-expression. We can learn to see the world with a poet's eye, noticing the subtle details and hidden beauty that often go unnoticed in the rush of daily life. We can learn to express our own thoughts and feelings with greater clarity and precision, drawing inspiration from the rich vocabulary of both visual and literary art. This process of creative exploration can be deeply rewarding, offering a pathway to self-discovery and a deeper connection to the world around us. It encourages us to embrace the power of observation, to cultivate our imaginations, and to find our own unique voice within the ongoing conversation of art. This enduring dialogue between poetry and painting offers a constant source of inspiration, reminding us of the transformative power of creative expression and its capacity to enrich our lives in countless ways. The symphony continues, inviting us to participate, to listen, to learn, and to create our own harmonious contributions to the ongoing conversation.

7.4 Bridging the Arts

The convergence of poetry and painting isn't merely an exercise in aesthetic appreciation; it's a dynamic interplay, a cross-pollination of creative energies that enriches both mediums. Think of it as building a bridge, not just admiring the chasm it spans. This bridge facilitates a deeper understanding of the artistic process itself, revealing shared concerns with composition, form, and emotional expression, regardless of the chosen medium. By exploring how poets and painters grapple with similar artistic challenges, we gain a more nuanced appreciation for the creative spirit in its myriad forms. We begin to see the common threads woven through seemingly disparate disciplines, recognizing the universal language of art that transcends specific techniques and materials.

This interconnectedness offers a unique opportunity for artistic growth. For painters, delving into poetry can spark new approaches to visual storytelling. The evocative imagery and rhythmic cadences of a poem can suggest novel compositions, color palettes, and thematic explorations. Consider how the compressed language of haiku, with its focus on natural imagery and evocative juxtaposition, might inspire a minimalist landscape painting. Or how the sweeping narrative of an epic poem could inform a series of interconnected canvases, each capturing a key moment in the story. The possibilities are as boundless as the imagination itself.

Conversely, poets can draw inspiration from the visual language of painting. Examining the brushstrokes, color choices, and compositional strategies of a master painter can unlock new avenues for poetic expression. The vibrant hues of a Van Gogh sunflower painting might inspire a poem exploring the emotional intensity of color. The dynamic lines and fragmented forms of a Cubist portrait could suggest a new approach to structuring a poem, using fragmented syntax and multiple perspectives to create a layered and complex portrait in words. This reciprocal exchange of ideas fuels creative innovation and pushes the boundaries of both mediums.

The act of translation itself, of moving between the verbal and the visual, is a powerful creative exercise. Attempting to capture the essence of a painting in words, or conversely, to translate a poem into a visual representation, forces us to grapple with the core elements of each art form. We must distill the complex interplay of color, light, and form into concise and evocative language, or conversely, find visual equivalents for the rhythms, metaphors, and emotional nuances of a poem. This process of distillation and transformation can lead to surprising insights and unexpected artistic breakthroughs.

Moreover, the bridge between poetry and painting fosters a deeper understanding of the audience's experience. Both poets and painters strive to evoke emotional responses, to create works that resonate with viewers and readers on a visceral level. By studying how each medium achieves this, artists can refine their own techniques for engaging their audience. A painter might learn from a poet's use of metaphor and symbolism to create a painting that speaks to deeper themes and emotions. A poet might draw inspiration from a painter's use of composition and perspective to create a poem that guides the reader's eye and controls the flow of information.

Ultimately, bridging the arts through the combined study of poetry and painting cultivates a more holistic approach to creativity. It encourages us to see the world through multiple lenses, to appreciate the nuances of both visual and verbal language, and to recognize the underlying unity that connects all forms of artistic expression. This expanded perspective not only enriches our appreciation of art but also empowers us to become more creative and insightful individuals, capable of expressing ourselves in more nuanced and meaningful ways. This symbiotic relationship is not a mere academic exercise but a vibrant and essential component of the creative process itself. It's a continuous dialogue, a conversation between forms that expands the possibilities of both and enriches the cultural landscape as a whole. By embracing this interconnectedness, we unlock the full potential of artistic expression and deepen our understanding of the human experience.

7.5 The Power of Synthesis

The culmination of our journey through the interwoven landscapes of poetry and painting brings us to the potent concept of synthesis. This isn't merely a blending, a simple mix of two mediums, but a true fusion, a chemical reaction where the individual elements—words and images—transform into something entirely new and greater than the sum of their parts. Think of it as the forging of a new alloy, stronger and more resilient than its constituent metals. This synthesis isn't about illustration or literal representation. We're not simply describing a painting with a poem, or painting a scene directly from a verse. Instead, we're seeking the deeper resonance, the shared emotional core, the underlying principles that unite these seemingly disparate forms. We are, in essence, creating a third entity, a new artistic experience born from the interplay of word and image.

This act of synthesis can take many forms. It might involve echoing the color palette of a painting in the descriptive language of a poem, mirroring the vibrant blues and fiery oranges of a Van Gogh landscape in the emotional intensity of the verse. Or perhaps it's replicating the rhythmic structure of a musical piece in both the meter of a poem and the dynamic composition of a painting, creating a unified sensory experience that transcends the limitations of each individual art form. Consider the sweeping curves and delicate lines of Art Nouveau, echoed in the flowing syntax and ornate imagery of a symbolist poem. The visual rhythm is translated into a literary one, creating a harmonious dialogue between the two works. The aim is not imitation, but a deeper exploration of shared artistic principles, finding resonance in form, feeling, and even philosophical underpinnings.

Another facet of synthesis lies in exploring the shared conceptual space between poetry and painting. Both artists grapple with themes of time, memory, identity, and the human condition. A poem exploring the ephemeral nature of time might find a visual counterpart in a painting depicting the fading light of a day, or the decay of an ancient ruin. The poem might not describe the painting directly, but both works can explore the same concept from their respective perspectives, enriching our understanding of the theme through multiple lenses. Consider a poem reflecting on the isolation of urban life. This could be synthesized with a painting depicting a lone figure amidst a bustling cityscape, not necessarily a literal depiction of the poem, but a visual echo of its core emotion. The painting amplifies the poem's sense of solitude, while the poem provides a narrative context for the painting's stark imagery.

Synthesis, importantly, also involves the audience. The viewer/reader becomes an active participant in this fusion, drawing connections, interpreting the interplay, and creating their own unique experience. A painting might spark a poem, or a poem might inspire a new way of seeing a painting. This interactive element further elevates the synthesis, transforming it from a static interplay between two works into a dynamic, ever-evolving conversation. Imagine encountering a painting depicting a stormy seascape. This image might inspire a poem capturing not just the visual elements of the scene, but also the emotional turmoil it evokes, the sense of vulnerability and awe in the face of nature's power. The viewer, having experienced both the visual and the literary interpretation, develops a richer, more nuanced understanding of the underlying theme.

Ultimately, the power of synthesis lies in its ability to transcend the limitations of individual art forms and create a more holistic, immersive, and ultimately more meaningful artistic experience. It's about finding the common ground, the shared language, the underlying principles that connect these seemingly disparate mediums. By exploring these connections, we unlock new layers of meaning, new avenues for creative expression, and a deeper appreciation for the interconnectedness of all art. It is in this synthesis, this harmonious fusion, that we truly begin to appreciate the full expressive potential of both poetry and painting, enriching not just our understanding of art, but our understanding of the world itself. The synthesis is the final brushstroke, the concluding stanza, the moment where the symphony of words and images reaches its crescendo, resonating with a power and beauty that transcends the individual notes and hues. It's the ultimate testament to the power of art to illuminate, to inspire, and to connect us to something larger than ourselves. This is the true legacy of the lyrical canvas.

www.ingramcontent.com/pod-product-compliance
Ingram Content Group UK Ltd.
Pitfield, Milton Keynes, MK11 3LW, UK
UKHW021436240125
4283UKWH00041B/637

9 798348 425197